Pocket Guide to Gilbert and Sullivan

D1353091

Pocket Guide to Gilbert and Sullivan

Jon Sutherland
and
Diane Canwell

REMEMBER WHEN

First published in Great Britain in 2011 by
REMEMBER WHEN
an imprint of
Pen & Sword Books Ltd
47 Church Street
Barnsley
South Yorkshire
S70 2AS

Copyright © Jon Sutherland and Diane Canwell 2011

ISBN 978 1 84468 103 7

The right of Jon Sutherland and Diane Canwell to be identified as authors
of this work has been asserted by them in accordance with the Copyright,
Designs and Patents Act 1988.

A CIP catalogue record for this book is
available from the British Library.

All rights reserved. No part of this book may be reproduced or transmitted
in any form or by any means, electronic or mechanical including
photocopying, recording or by any information storage and retrieval system,
without permission from the Publisher in writing.

Printed and bound in the UK by CPI

Pen & Sword Books Ltd incorporates the imprints of Pen & Sword Aviation,
Pen & Sword Maritime, Pen & Sword Military, Wharncliffe Local History,
Pen & Sword Select, Pen & Sword Military Classics, Leo Cooper, Remember
When, Seaforth Publishing and Frontline Publishing

For a complete list of Pen & Sword titles please contact
PEN & SWORD BOOKS LIMITED
47 Church Street, Barnsley, South Yorkshire, S70 2AS, England
E-mail: enquiries@pen-and-sword.co.uk
Website: www.pen-and-sword.co.uk

Contents

DUDLEY PUBLIC LIBRARIES	
000000467054	
Bertrams	19/04/2011
782.120922	£12.99
	ST

Introduction

William Schwenck Gilbert and Arthur Seymour Sullivan collaborated on 14 comic operas, some of which would become the most frequently performed works in musical theatre. They continue to be staged across the world.

The two men also had their own prodigious output of plays, stories, lyrics and music. Their style and approach would influence generations of musicians and dramatists, such as George Bernard Shaw and Oscar Wilde.

The relationship between Gilbert and Sullivan was not always an easy one. They began working together in 1871 and at their peak in the late 1870s and 1880s they would produce a series of extremely successful comic operas, with a new one appearing every year or two. The two men were radically different characters, however, and they often quarrelled over issues such as subject matter, politics and expenses. Throughout the relationship was a very fragile one. By the 1890s the partnership was virtually at an end, after more arguments about artistes, amendments to storylines and lyrics.

Their legacy was not just in the operas themselves, but also in bricks and mortar. The Savoy Theatre had been built specifically to accommodate their operas and Gilbert had gone on to build the Garrick Theatre in 1889. Sullivan was knighted in 1883 and Gilbert in 1907. Their innovations were a direct influence on the musicals that would follow; many of their techniques provided a model for lyricists working on Broadway.

Another enduring legacy was the composers' relationship with Richard D'Oyly Carte. From 1875 he had produced and managed many of their greatest operas, culminating in the construction of the Savoy Theatre in 1882. Although D'Oyly Carte died in 1901, his name would also live on, inextricably linked to that of Gilbert and Sullivan, as The

D'Oyly Carte Opera Company, which continues to exist and to perform Gilbert and Sullivan works to this day.

On a personal note, researching this book has taken me back 40 years to the Sadler's Wells Theatre, on Rosebery Avenue in London, recalling the annual arrival of the D'Oyly Carte Company and managing the packed auditorium before curtain up. Each season brought with it a new mix of the operas. By the end of each tour every line of each verse and every theatrical nuance was so familiar that one felt one was a part of the company itself.

Chapter 1

Who Were Gilbert and Sullivan?

Gilbert and Sullivan would become the fathers of the modern blockbuster musical. They created a formula that almost guaranteed theatrical success. Their musicals were melodic and funny and they would continue to attract literally millions of fans to this very day. It was one of the first musical marriages; an artistic partnership, a testing one for the pair of them, and one that was often punctuated with disputes and quarrels. Yet their partnership would become the blueprint for the Gershwins, Rodgers and Hammerstein, and Lloyd Webber and Rice, to name but a few. Gilbert and Sullivan created 14 light operas and so popular would they become that they have been, and continue to be, performed by professional and amateur groups across the world.

William Schwenck Gilbert (1836–1911)

His early life

Gilbert was born in the house of his grandfather, at 17 Southampton Street in London. His father was a naval surgeon and his mother was the daughter of a doctor. He had three younger sisters; Jane, Maud and Florence. They lived at 4 Portland Place in Hammersmith and at the age of two Gilbert, whilst being looked after by a maid, was kidnapped in Naples, his parents paying £25 for his safe return. Interestingly, child kidnap would be part of the plots of *HMS Pinafore*, *The Gondoliers* and *The Pirates of Penzance*, so the experience obviously left an indelible mark on him.

Gilbert's parents separated when he was 19 and it seems clear that he did not come from a particularly happy home. Again shades of his upbringing often emerged in the work that he would write later in life. When Gilbert was seven he was at school in Boulogne and was a fluent French speaker. By the age of 13 he was at Great Ealing School.

A portrait of Gilbert by Frank Holl dated 1886, which hangs in the National Portrait Gallery.

In Gilbert's own words:

"He speedily won the reputation of being a clever, bright boy, who was extremely lazy. It was soon discovered, however, that he could work so quickly that his natural tendency to idleness was no handicap to his abilities."

He was at a school that had taught distinguished writers such as Huxley and Thackeray. Out of school he was interested in drawing and reading, but he was already fascinated by the theatre. Again Gilbert said:

"Under the influence of social intercourse with many literary and theatrical friends who frequented his father's house, his bias for the stage naturally entered largely into his ambitions."

Gilbert played Guy Fawkes in a melodrama at school and when he was 15 he saw the actor Charles Kean in *The Corsican Brothers*. Kean knew Gilbert's father and sent him back to school when Gilbert turned up at the theatre and asked him for a job.

By the age of 16 Gilbert had become head boy at his school and was also fluent in Latin and Greek. He loved reading Edward Lear and Charles Dickens. After Great Ealing School, Gilbert went to King's College, London, to study law in 1853. He also decided that he would try to get a commission in the Royal Artillery. He was fascinated by the Crimean War and uniforms; this would be another enduring part of the operas that he would write in the future. At this stage Gilbert fully intended to become a soldier:

> "When I was 19 years old, the Crimean War was at its height, and commissions in the Royal Artillery were thrown open to competitive examination. So I read for the examination for direct commissions, which was to be held at Christmas 1856. The limit of the age was 20, and as at the date of examination I should have been six weeks over that age, I applied for and obtained from Lord Panmure, the then Secretary of State for War, a dispensation for this excess, and worked away with a will. But the war came to a rather abrupt and unexpected end, and no more officers being required, the examination was indefinitely postponed. Among the blessings of peace may be reckoned certain comedies, operas, farces, and extravaganzas which, if the war had lasted another six weeks, would in all probability never have been written."

First artistic efforts

By October 1855 Gilbert was a student at Inner Temple, studying law. In 1857 he finished his degree and sat an examination to enter the civil service. He became a clerk in the education department of the Privy Council. From the outset he found the job extremely dull and used the ridiculous situations and bureaucracy as a backdrop for his sketches.

Gilbert became a part-time officer in the 5th West Yorkshire Militia. By 1865 he was in the Royal Aberdeenshire Militia, with the rank of captain.

His first work in print was a translation of the Promenade Concert programmes, which gave him an appetite to see his name in print again. By the time he was 24 he had written 15 theatrical works; each time they were rejected.

In 1860 Gilbert inherited £300 from an aunt and gave up his civil service job, was called to the bar and began work as a barrister. He joined the Northern Circuit after working in London courts and first appeared as a prosecutor in Liverpool. This job was no more appealing to Gilbert than the last; he had few clients and over the four years or so was more interested in sketching situations in the court room than practising law. Each of these experiences filled his mind with ideas and his knowledge of the law would also make an appearance in later operas.

In 1861 the magazine *Fun* was first published and Gilbert was commissioned to write articles and provide drawings. He also wrote poems, not just for *Fun* but also for *Punch*. He called his poems the *Bab Ballads* and in 1869 a collection of these were published, followed by a second volume in 1873. In 1877 Gilbert selected the best of the ballads for another book. Altogether there were 139 poems, but these were never published in one book until the 1970s.

Gilbert also illustrated works that had been written by his father and it seemed for a time that Gilbert's career would lay in writing and creating ballads. He married Lucy Agnes Turner in 1867; she was 17 and the daughter of an army officer. They lived in Kensington and they would remain together for the rest of their lives.

By the middle of 1869 Gilbert seems to have tired of his poems and had a new interest in dramas. He had already written the burlesque *Dulcamara* in 1866, but *The Palace of Truth* met with considerable success in 1870. The Haymarket Theatre also staged *Pygmalion and Galatea*; this was incredibly successful and including the revivals would earn Gilbert £40,000. Gilbert had finally found something that he not only enjoyed but was also profitable. Over the years he would also plunder his back catalogue of ballads, poems and other writings to provide material for his operas.

Gilbert was always open about the relationship between the ballads and his operas and indeed the influence of other writers' work, which he often adapted to form the basis of one of the operas. Slowly but surely Gilbert was becoming more and more skilled; he had learned from

The music cover for the dance arrangement of Cox and Box.

experience and his drawing skills would be of enormous value to him in the future years, as he was also able to create costumes and scenes.

1867 would in fact be an incredibly important year, not just for Gilbert but also for Sullivan. Gilbert reviewed Sullivan's first comic opera, *Cox and Box*, which was being performed at the Adelphi Theatre. Gilbert wrote:

> "Mr Sullivan's music is, in many places, of too high a class for the grotesquely absurd plot to which it is wedded. It is funny here and there, and grand or graceful where it is not funny; but the grand and the graceful have, we think, too large a share of the honours to themselves."

In fact Gilbert's comments would underline a major bone of contention that would continue throughout his working life with Sullivan: the fact that the music was too dominating and that it submerged the words and plot.

Arthur Seymour Sullivan (1842–1900)

His early life

Sullivan was born at 8 Bolwell Terrace in Lambeth, London on May 13 1842. His father, Thomas, was of Irish stock and was a clarinet player in theatres. His mother, Maria Clementina Coughlan, has been variously described as being of Italian or Jewish origins. Sullivan had an older brother Frederic and from the outset the pair of them were encouraged to take an interest in music. In fact in the early years Sullivan's father taught and copied out music to supplement his income.

There were also military traditions in the family; Sullivan's grandfather had been a British soldier and had served during the Napoleonic Wars. Sullivan also recalled the story that his grandfather became the paymaster of Napoleon's household after his surrender in 1815 and that after Napoleon died, in 1821, his grandfather sat in the room where Napoleon's body was laid out, with a musket in his hand to shoot any rats that might appear.

In the early years Thomas Sullivan played the clarinet at the Surrey Theatre and then became bandmaster at the Royal Military College at Sandhurst. This effectively took them out of relative poverty and by the

The opening of the Great Industrial Exhibition at Crystal Palace in 1861. From the Library of Congress collection

age of eight Sullivan was becoming relatively proficient at nearly all of the instruments in his father's band. Sullivan also had an excellent singing voice and with the help of a close family friend he managed to join the Chapel Royal Choir. It was a small and exclusive group that sang at the services in the Royal palaces and they also performed on state occasions. They lived in their own private boarding school at 6 Cheyne Walk in Chelsea.

Sullivan became the first boy to sing solo at the christening of one of Queen Victoria's children, was patted on the head by the Duke of Wellington, rewarded with a half sovereign from the Prince Consort and performed at the Crystal Palace, along with the Grenadier Guards and Coldstream Guards. It was also clear that Sullivan had his own musical talent in writing and before he was 13 he saw his first music published.

At the age of 14 Sullivan applied for the Mendelssohn Scholarship and won it in 1856. This enabled him to attend the Royal Academy of Music. After sitting an examination the following year his scholarship was renewed. He showed enormous potential and it was decided that he would go to Leipzig to continue his musical education. This meant becoming a

Mendelssohn scholar for a third year. Sullivan arrived in Leipzig in September 1858; it had a tremendous reputation and the 16- year-old boy thrived.

First artistic efforts

By 1860 Sullivan's days at Leipzig seemed to be coming to a close. The Sullivan family managed to raise extra money when his father gave lessons at the piano makers, Broadwoods. Sullivan was also relieved of the need to pay tuition fees and he eventually returned to London in the summer of 1861, thoroughly trained and ready to write music. In fact while he was in Leipzig he had written music for *The Tempest*. This was picked up by George Groves, who put on the performance of *The Tempest* at the Crystal Palace in 1862. Queen Victoria asked Sullivan to compose a *Te Deum* in honour of the marriage of the Prince of Wales. Sullivan also became Master of the Queen's Music.

Sullivan taught at the Chapel Royal and became Professor of Pianoforte and Ballad Singing at the Crystal Palace School of Art. He continued writing and also became the organist at St Michael's Church in Chester Square.

Portrait of Arthur Sullivan by Milais dated 1888. It hangs next to Frank Holl's portrait of W S Gilbert in the National Portrait Gallery.

Towards the end of 1862 Sullivan went to Paris with Charles Dickens, the Lehmanns and Henry Fothergill Chorley. Here Sullivan met the composer Rossini and together they played duets from *The Tempest*. Sullivan was to be deeply influenced by Rossini's style, along with Schubert and Mendelssohn. In 1864 he wrote a ballet, *L'ile Enchantée*, for Covent Garden. He became the theatre's organist, but his own first opera, *The Sapphire Necklace*, was not performed. Sullivan then wrote a cantata for the Birmingham Festival, along with Chorley. He was back in Vienna in October 1867 as an assistant to George Groves before meeting Clara Schumann in Baden-Baden.

Back in Vienna, Sullivan met the nephew of Schubert and worked to complete *Rosamunde* with lost symphonies by Schubert, which were performed in November 1867 at Crystal Palace. From 1867 to 1872 Sullivan was the organist at St Peter's Church in Cranley Gardens. A year earlier he had written a symphony and a cello concerto. In 1869 he wrote *The Prodigal Son* for the Worcester Festival and in the following year *Overture di Ballo* for the Birmingham Festival. By now Sullivan was also a professor of composition at the Royal Academy of Music and towards the end of the decade he moved to Pimlico, where Gilbert also lived. Sullivan also composed a number of hymn tunes, most of which were published, his most famous tune being *Onward Christian Soldiers*. Sullivan had gained many of his contacts through extensive networking and his close association with George Groves.

He had affairs with two of John Scott Russell's daughters, Rachel and Louise, in the 1860s. In fact he secretly became engaged to Rachel. Sullivan's father had died in October 1866, but his father's death had proved to be the catalyst to create the critically acclaimed oratorio *In Memoriam*, which was performed at the Norwich Festival the same month. Rachel would eventually marry and move to India, where she died at the age of 36 in 1882 and although she burned all of the letters that Sullivan sent to her, he kept all her letters. Louise died of consumption as a spinster in 1878.

Sullivan was fast becoming one of the most popular composers in England; his work was routinely performed at major music festivals across Britain. In the early 1870s he produced many major works and his first opera, *Cox and Box*, was performed with lyrics written by Francis Burnand. With Gilbert having watched and reviewed the opera, the scene was now set for them to meet. Everything that the pair had achieved independently up until this point paled into insignificance once the two entered into their eternal partnership.

Gilbert meets Sullivan

Leslie Baily wrote of their meeting:

> "One morning in 1869 a cab drew up at the Royal Gallery of Illustration and Mr Sullivan stepped out with Mr Frederick Clay. Sullivan at this period was a short, rather squat young man, beautifully dressed in frock coat and tall hat, with glossy black hair and side whiskers, an eye glass, and a jaunty manner. Two years had passed since the failure of his comic opera *The Contrabandista*; Frederick Clay is known to posterity merely for his ballad *I'll Sing Thee Songs of Araby*, but he was a frequent composer for the German Reed Entertainment [German Reed was putting on a performance at the Gallery of Illustration] and so on this particular day in 1869 he invited Sullivan to come in and watch a rehearsal of his latest piece, *Ages Ago*. The score of this work carries the line 'dedicated to Arthur Sullivan'. The author was W S Gilbert, who had been contributing short dramatic pieces to the German Reed Entertainment for some time."

The two men were introduced and Gilbert asked Sullivan a complex musical question to which Sullivan had no immediate answer. It was Gilbert's way of teasing Sullivan. It is possible that these events took place on July 11 1870, on a Monday afternoon. This would have been the final rehearsal for *Ages Ago*, which had ended its run in June 1870 and was then being revised for reopening.

Their paths would cross again, but it was clear that they were two completely different people, with very different temperaments. They had little in common and although they would work together they would never really become friends. The stage was definitely being set, however, for the two men to begin working together. Mutual friends and acquaintances would push the two men closer until collaboration became the inevitable conclusion. In the meantime, however, the pair would continue to work independently until the world was presented with their first collaboration, *Thespis: The Gods Grown Old*.

Chapter 2

The First Collaborations

For the time being the pair continued to work on their independent careers. Gilbert produced *Our Island Home*. Themes in this piece would recur when he wrote *The Pirates of Penzance* and *HMS Pinafore*. He also wrote *A Sensation Novel* and *Happy Arcadia*. His most successful comedy of the six that were performed in London in 1871 was *Pygmalion and Galatea*, which ran at the Haymarket for over 200 performances. Other pieces from this period, such as *No Cards*, had a

1905 oil painting by J Andre Castaigne of the New Gaiety Theatre in London. From the Library of Congress collection.

striking resemblance to *Patience*, which he would later produce with Sullivan and *Ruddigore* had ideas taken from *Ages Ago*. Gilbert was also writing a number of short stories for magazines. Meanwhile Sullivan continued to write ballads. But the first collaboration was at hand.

John Hollingshead had opened the Gaiety Theatre, in the Strand, in 1868. On the opening night Gilbert's play *Robert the Devil* had been performed and Sullivan was in the audience. In late 1871 Hollingshead approached Gilbert to write a comic opera for Christmas. He also suggested Sullivan as the ideal choice to write the score. This was not the first time that the pair had been put together by others; in fact the German Reeds had asked Sullivan to work with Gilbert on a joint production in 1870, but due to pressure of work Sullivan had turned this down. This time the pair would work together.

Gilbert wrote the libretto and Sullivan had finished writing the music by the December. The opera was read to the company in mid-December and this gave them two weeks to put the production together, as it would open on Boxing Day.

Thespis

Thespis was a two act opera based on the Gods of Olympus. A theatrical troupe had found their way to Mount Olympus. A review written in *The Times* on December 27, 1871 described the piece:

"The after piece – Christmas piece, or pantomime, would be a word hardly in keeping with the stand-point of the Gaiety Theatre – is what in Paris would be known as an *Opera Bouffe*, which in English may be freely rendered as an opera grotesque. The name *Thespis, or the Gods grown old*, reveals its character. The plot turns upon the decay of veneration for the old heathen deities, and the incongruities attendant upon a restoration, even for stage purposes, of the Temple of Olympus. The dialogue throughout is superior in ability and point to that with which ordinary burlesque and extravaganzas have familiarized us; so much so, in fact, that it was a daring experiment to produce such a piece on such a night. It met, however, with an excellent reception, and on any other occasion than Boxing-night the numerous merits of the piece cannot fail to secure for it in public estimation a high place among the novelties of the season. The opera, for which the merit of entire originality is claimed, has been written by Mr. W. S. Gilbert, and the music composed by Mr. Arthur Sullivan. In honour of the occasion, Mr. Sullivan conducted the orchestra in person, and was warmly applauded on taking his seat for that purpose.

The curtain rises upon Mount Olympus, or rather upon a fog on Mount Olympus, from the midst of which Diana (Mrs H. Leigh) and her attendant train emerging are heard loud in complaint of the hardship of their lot in keeping nightly watch in such unseasonable weather. Apollo (Mr. F. Sullivan), an elderly dandy, in his turn laments the necessity of exertion, and declares his intention of 'not going out at all that day.' Jupiter (Mr. J. Maclean) and Mars (Mr. Wood), regular club notables of a bygone age, similarly shirk from trouble of any kind, and lament the degeneracy of the age; but all with a well-bred languid air, as if of feeling bored by the continued discharge of duties to which mankind no longer attached their former significance. Mercury alone (Miss E. Farren) retains vivacity enough for all Olympus, and humorously bewails the unkind fate which credits others with the performance of work in reality accomplished by the Olympian drudge herself.

The conclave is interrupted by the arrival of a band of pedestrians who have actually selected the sacred Mount as the site for a pic-nic, and unaffrighted by the nods and frowns, and even the thunderings of mighty Jove himself, proceed to take possession. These are members of the travelling theatrical company of Thespis (Mr. Toole), who, being invited, as he himself describes it, to 'confer with a brother manager' gravely suggests that his party and the gods should change places, and the latter should visit earth for a year, and see with their own eyes how matters there are going on. It will be hardly necessary to suggest how, in the interval, things run riot; though Mr. Toole, on the return of the Deities, labours hard to convince them that everything and everybody is going on just as usual – 'except the Tichborne trial, which has got a fortnight.'

The Thespian company includes every shade of character – Bacchus, who takes the pledge – the substitute Diana, who won't go out at night without an escort – two agile members of the Payne family as Preposteros and Stupidas, and numberless fair members

An engraving from The Graphic *of a rehearsal of* Thespis *dated 1871 to identify the missing movements of the piece.*

who dance and sing, make love and quarrel in most celestial fashion, though not in all cases in strict accordance with Lempriere. The dresses, as usual at this theatre, are brilliant and becoming, and the music, to which only a passing reference can now be made, was animated and full of airs to be remembered. The ballet in the second act seemed a little out of place, and the *finale* somewhat wanting in the spirit which marked the remainder of the piece; but these, doubtless, were matters incident to a first reproduction. The piece, as a whole, deserves high praise."

Thespis Original Cast and Synopsis

GODS
Jupiter	John Maclean
Apollo	Frederic Sullivan
Mars	Frank Wood

Diana	Mrs H Leigh
Mercury	Ellen Farren
Venus	Miss Jolly

THESBIANS

Thespis	J L Toole
Sillimon	J G Taylor
Timidon	Mr Marshall
Tipseion	Robert Soutar
Preposteros	Henry Payne
Stupidas	Fred Payne
Sparkeion	Mlle. Clary
Nicemis	Constance Loseby
Pretteia	Rose Berend
Daphne	Annie Tremaine
Cymon	Miss L Wilson

Detail from an engraving of the pantomimes of 1871 showing a scene from Thespis, *where Thespis first meets the Gods.*

The subtitle was *The Gods Grown Old* and it was billed as a grotesque opera. It ran for 64 performances.

Act I – A ruined temple on the summit of Olympus
Olympus is in ruins and the Gods look old and rely on hair products, cosmetics and drugs to keep themselves presentable. The root cause is the fact that their popularity has dwindled. Suddenly mortals appear, including the two young lovers Sparkeion and Nicemis, who are getting married that day. Initially the Gods hide and then Jupiter scares away the mortals. But Thespis introduces himself to Jupiter. Jupiter asks him why people no longer worship the Gods and Thespis recommends that the Gods visit earth to find out. Thespis also offers his troupe of performers as replacements for the Gods whilst they visit earth. Mercury is left behind to keep an eye on things.

Act II – The same scene as Act I, but with the ruins restored
A year later and the theatrical troupe have moved in. There have been major problems and the actors have not been very good at assigning jobs to one another. In fact everything has gone to rack and ruin, with the stand-in Gods forgetting to carry out even the most basic jobs. The Gods rouse themselves and evict the actors. The actors are punished to become

An illustration by D H Friston from The Illustrated London News, *showing* Thespis. *The scene is of Act I, just after the Gods appear to Thespis.*

a troupe of performers that no one ever goes to see and the Gods are left to sort out the problems that have been left behind by the actors.

It was not an entirely satisfactory opening for the new partnership; Sullivan moaned that very few of the actors could actually sing. The opera was not that well received and at times the audience booed the performance and there were snags that meant that the performance often ran late. In fact it was past midnight when the performance was over.

Nonetheless there were bright points in the performance and critics could see that the two men complimented one another very well. Sixty four performances was a reasonably respectable run, particularly for an opera that was only designed to run over the festive period.

The music to *Thespis* has largely disappeared, probably because Gilbert found this first collaboration to be something of an embarrassment.

From The Graphic, *dated February 10 1872. This shows a scene near the end of You're Diane, I'm Apollo. Original by H Woods.*

Sullivan certainly used some of the music for other operas; it was another example of the recycling of material.

After *Thespis* finished its run the two men would go their separate ways again and it would be another three years before they would work together once more.

Gilbert would spend the next four years writing and producing plays; not all of them met with success. Gilbert's version of the Faustian legend *Gretchen* closed within a fortnight. He also sued the *Pall Mall Gazette* during this time and lost the case after they condemned one of his pieces based on a short story he had written, *The Wicked World*. Gilbert wrote a broad range of different pieces; *The Sentimental Sweethearts*, the comedy *Topsy-Turveydom* and the melodramatic, *On Bail*. He wrote a three-act farce, which was performed at the St James's Theatre, *Tom Cobb* and *Ne'er Do Well*, which in Gilbert's own words was a failure for the Olympic Theatre, as well *Broken Hearts* for the Court Theatre. In Gilbert's words:

> "I consider the two best plays I ever wrote were *Broken Hearts* and a version of the Faust legend called *Gretchen*. I took immense pains over my *Gretchen*, but it only ran a fortnight. I wrote it to please myself, and not the public."

Amongst the failures, however, there were success stories, like the 1873 *The Wedding March*. He earned around £2,500 for a day and a half's work, adapting it from the French and reducing it to three acts. Gilbert was something of a celebrity by this stage and was now living at 24 The Boltons in Kensington.

The actress and singer Ellaline Terriss said of Gilbert in these years:

> "He was a great stage manager and could show you what he meant by acting a scene for you. Sometimes having to impersonate a girl's part, being six feet in height and big in proportion, he seemed funny, but he wasn't really, for he conveyed even to the ladies the exact way his dialogue should be spoken."

There was also an odd situation when a new writer, F. Tomline, wrote a parody of Gilbert's *The Wicked World*, called *The Happy Land*. It transpired that Tomline was in fact Gilbert. *The Happy Land* had impersonations of leading government ministers and it was banned. But Gilbert made a few changes and it ran for 200 nights at the Court Theatre.

German Reed had retired in 1871 and his work at the Royal Gallery of Illustration was taken over by his son, Cecil. He opened at St George's Hall with *Ages Ago* and amongst the cast was Leonora Braham, who would become one of the stars of the Savoy Opera. There was also a taste of what was to come in *The Yeoman of the Guard*, when Gilbert wrote with F. Pascal, *Eyes and No Eyes* for Reed. It began with a girl singing at a spinning wheel.

Sullivan, meanwhile, had written *The Light of the World* in 1873 and it was much loved by Queen Victoria. It was first performed in Birmingham and John Hollingshead had Sullivan write the incidental music for *The Merry Wives of Windsor* at the Gaiety Theatre. It was first performed in 1874, but Sullivan was unwell, suffering from kidney stones, a complaint that was to last for the rest of his life.

Another man was about to enter Gilbert and Sullivan's life and throw them together once again. He became an integral part of their most productive and successful years. He was Richard D'Oyly Carte.

Richard D'Oyly Carte (1844-1901)

Richard D'Oyly Carte was born in Soho on May 3, 1844. He was the son of Richard Carte, a flute player and partner in a business that made musical instruments. His mother was the daughter of a clergyman, she was well travelled and this would be a feature of Richard D'Oyly Carte's life. They spoke fluent French and after D'Oyly Carte left University College he joined the family business.

It is interesting to note that the D'Oyly part of his name was in fact a second Christian name and the name was not actually double-barrelled. D'Oyly Carte composed songs and wrote music. By 1870 he had opened his own concert and operatic agency near Charring Cross. He organised singers' and lecturers' tours and was a strong supporter of English opera. He had by this stage realised that his own musical talents were limited, but he was an excellent manager; shrewd and with a keen business sense.

D'Oyly Carte had seen *Thespis* and could see the potential of Gilbert and Sullivan. He was 31 when he brought the 33-year-old Sullivan and 39-year-old Gilbert together again. The result would be *Trial by Jury*.

An engraving from The Illustrated Sporting *and* Dramatic News *of Gilbert and Sullivan's* Trial by Jury, *dated May 1875.*

At the beginning of 1875 Selina Dolaro, the English actress, singer, theatre manager and writer, had leased the Royalty Theatre in Dean Street, London. D'Oyly Carte was her business manager. Part of the performance would be worked by Offenbach and it occurred to D'Oyly Carte that he should get Gilbert and Sullivan together to write something specifically for the second part of the evening's entertainment.

Gilbert had already shown D'Oyly Carte a libretto called *Trial by Jury*. The plan had been originally to set it to music by Carl Rosa, but Carl Rosa's wife had died in 1874 and nothing had come of it. D'Oyly Carte was still keen to put on the opera and told Gilbert that he wanted Sullivan to write the music. It was to be a momentous meeting.

Gilbert and D'Oyly Carte went to Sullivan's house and Gilbert read the libretto to him. Sullivan later said:

"He read it through, as it seemed to me, in a perturbed sort of way, with a gradual crescendo of indignation, in the manner of a man considerably disappointed with what he had written. As soon as he had come to the last word he closed up the manuscript violently, apparently unconscious of the fact that he had achieved his purpose so far as I was concerned, in as much as I was screaming with laughter the whole time."

Sullivan loved it and dashed off the music in three weeks. In fact by the end of the three weeks it had even been rehearsed.

Trial by Jury

Trial by Jury was first performed at 10.15 p.m. on March 25, 1875 at the Royalty Theatre. Sullivan's older brother Fred played the Learned Judge.

The Times provided the first night review, published on March 29, 1875:

"A description of Mr. Gilbert's piece would answer little purpose, inasmuch as it defies analysis. It is a harmless 'skit' upon the adjudiacture of a case for 'breach of promise', in the course of which the twelve members of the Jury and the enlightened Judge himself become so fascinated with the personal attractions of the Plaintiff Angelina that all chance for the Defendant is gone at the very instant the fair deceived one makes her appearance. The upshot is that, at a crisis when the jury are unable to come to an understanding, the Judge, impatient, suddenly descending from the bench, to cut the matter short, embraces Plaintiff (Angelina nothing loth) and declares he will marry her himself.

The music of Mr. Sullivan, without reference to purely artistic merits which can hardly fail to strike connoisseurs, is precisely what, under the circumstances, it should be. Composed of slighter material than that of *Cox and Box*, and more particularly of the *Contrabandista*, it is, in its way, just as good and just as effective as either. No situation has been overlooked in which the music can be made comically subservient to the dramatic purport of Mr. [Gilbert. Mr.] Sullivan, in fact, has accomplished his part in the extravaganza so happily that – to ascend some steps higher towards the Empyrean – it seems, as in the great Wagnerian operas, as though poem and music had proceeded simultaneously from one and the same brain. There is genuine humour – as, for instance, in the unison chorus of the jury-men, and the clever parody on one of the most renowned finales of modern Italian opera; and there is also melody, both fluent and catching, here and there, moreover, set off by little touches in the orchestral accompaniments which reveal the experienced hand.

The performance of *Trial by Jury*, if exhibiting occasional shortcomings which closer familiarity may help to set right, is

Gilbert's original draft of Trial by Jury, *as a short comic piece, published in* Fun *in 1868.*

generally good. The orchestra, though numerically limited, is for the most part efficient; while the chief characters on the stage are carefully represented. Miss Nelly Bromley is a Plaintiff engaging enough to account for the predilection of Judge and Jury in her favour; Mr. F. Sullivan's impersonation of the learned and impressionable Judge deserves a special word of praise for its quiet and natural humour; Messrs. W. Fisher, Hollingsworth, and Pepper doing their best as Defendant, Plaintiff's Counsellor, and Usher of the Jury. It should be added that the various costumes are exact, without caricature, and that – the appearance of the Plaintiff with a troop of bridesmaids, in bridesmaids' attire excepted – everything is precisely what might be witnessed on such an occasion in the court at Westminster."

Many people consider that this is Gilbert and Sullivan's greatest work, although at the time even the posters put Sullivan's name forward and Gilbert's name to the back. D'Oyly Carte was probably simply playing on the relative fame of Sullivan compared to Gilbert.

It was the only opera that Gilbert and Sullivan wrote in one act. It is the shortest, running at around 40 minutes, and there is no spoken dialogue between the choruses and songs. Compared to the experiences of *Thespis*, they had had two months to prepare for the performance. Gilbert designed the set himself and his instructions were precise and clear. Sullivan also enjoyed his experience of working on *Trial by Jury*. He parodied other operas and his brother Fred had been a triumph too; his performance met with critical acclaim. Fred Sullivan, however, would die in his thirties at the beginning of 1877.

Trial by Jury Original Cast and Synopsis

The Learned Judge	Frederic Sullivan
Council for the Plaintiff	J Hollingsworth
The Defendant	Walter H Fisher
Forman of the Jury	C Campbell
Usher	C Kelleher
Associate	B R Pepper
Plaintiff	Nellie Bromley
Bridesmaids	Madame Verner, Amy Clifford, Villiers Lassalle, Madame Durrant,

	Madame Palmer, Julia Beverley and
	Madame Lee
Gentlemen of the Jury	Mr Bradshaw and Mr Husk

The length of the original run was for 131 performances.

This one-act play opens with the court waiting for the first case of the day. Angelina, the Plaintiff, is suing Edwin, the defendant, for breach of promise of a marriage. Edwin is subjected to abuse as he enters the court and tells his side of the story. He explains that in his youth he fell in love with Angelina, became bored with her and fell in love with someone else. The Learned Judge appears and tells the court about his career and how he promised to marry an elderly, ugly daughter of a wealthy lawyer. The

An original W S Gilbert Bab illustration to the judge's song. The original illustration dates around 1897.

lawyer helped the judge in his career and as soon as the judge was successful he dropped the lawyer's daughter, making him an ideal judge to oversee this case. The jury is sworn in and Angelina's bridesmaids enter. The judge sends a note to the leading bridesmaid and when Angelina appears he sends a note to her. Council puts Angelina's case and Angelina faints in court. Edwin defends himself and suggests that he will marry Angelina and then his new girlfriend the following day. The judge tells him that this is unlawful. Angelina tells the court how much she loves Edwin and wants compensation. Edwin tells the court that he both smokes and drinks to excess and has a temper, so she cannot love him. The legal proceedings come to a close when the judge proposes to Angelina himself and she accepts. The rest of the court concurs with this decision.

Why was *Trial by Jury* so successful?

Gilbert and Sullivan had learned a lot since the relative failure of *Thespis*. *Trial by Jury* had high standards of scenery and costume design, and in fact the costumes were graceful and colourful, having been heavily influenced by William Morris. It was also a period that was seeing the after effects of the Education Act (1870); there were more educated women, they were theatre goers and theatrical standards were improving. It was also a time when the British Empire was sparking with life; the world did not seem such a dull and dreary place after Disraeli succeeded Gladstone as prime minister. Gilbert had also made sure that the cast knew exactly what was required of them.

Straight after the run Sullivan worked as the conductor of the Glasgow Orchestral and Choral Union until 1877. He also met with the Duke of Edinburgh and the Prince of Wales, which led to the founding of the National Training School of Music, founded in May 1876. Sullivan became the principal, holding the post until 1881. This of course is now known as the Royal College of Music.

As soon as *Trial by Jury* was up and running D'Oyly Carte tried to get Gilbert and Sullivan together again to write a full-length comic opera. Gilbert was involved in producing the comedy *Engaged* for the Haymarket Theatre.

Trial by Jury's end did not come as a result of lack of interest, but in the illness of Fred Sullivan. Sullivan told the *Strand Musical Magazine* in 1895:

"I was nursing my brother through a severe illness and had hardly left his bedside for several days and nights. Finding one evening that he had fallen into a doze, I crept away into a room adjoining his, and tried to snatch a few minutes rest. I found this impossible,

Part of the original vocal score of Trial by Jury, *showing the complex vocal scoring. Published around 1875.*

however, so I roused myself to work, and made one more of many attempts during four years to set music to Adelaide Proctor's interesting words. This time I felt that the right inspiration had come to me at last, and there and then I composed *The Lost Chord*. That song was evolved under the most trying circumstances, and was the outcome of a very unhappy and troubled state of mind."

In fact *The Lost Chord* would become one of the most popular ballads of the entire century. People could hear it everywhere. It has sold hundreds of thousands of copies.

Gilbert had already pencilled Fred Sullivan in for the principle comedy part in a new opera, but Fred suddenly died, at the age of 39, on January 18 1877. Sullivan was inconsolable.

Chapter 3

The First Successes

Sullivan had spent the summer of 1875 at Lake Como and here he wrote his highly successful song *Let Me Dream Again*. After the death of his brother Sullivan's mother moved to Fulham to live with Fred's widow and children. Sullivan had also struck up a friendship with Mary Frances Ronalds, better known as Fanny Ronalds. In fact it is almost certain that she was his mistress. Mary was a talented singer and her recording of *The Lost Chord* was one of the first ever recordings made in England. She was also a close friend of the Prince of Wales and Princess Alexandra and she hosted Sullivan's dinner parties. Mary was 10 years older than Sullivan and played an important role in both his private and professional life.

Meanwhile Gilbert wrote works with Fred Clay, including *Princess Toto*. He also saw his plays *Broken Hearts, Charity, Sweethearts* and *Engaged* all produced in London.

In 1876 Richard D'Oyly Carte formed the Comedy Opera Company Limited. The four main backers were the music publisher George Metzler, a close associate of Metzler, Frank Chappell, the owner of a piano making company, Collard Augustus Drake, and Edward Hodgson Bayley, who owned a business that sprinkled water to keep down the dust on London streets. D'Oyly Carte became the general manager.

A number of principal writers were approached to write work for the company, but D'Oyly Carte really wanted Gilbert and Sullivan to produce something for him. With the promise of an advance of 200 guineas each when the words and music were delivered, Gilbert and Sullivan signed an agreement in July 1877 to create *The Sorcerer*. Gilbert delved into his back catalogue of work, selecting a short story that had appeared in *Graphic* called *An Elixir of Love*. It was about a love potion that a curate obtained from magicians in London to give out to his parishioners. It would feature unlikely couples falling in love after drinking spiked cups of tea.

By the spring of 1877 Gilbert had completed the libretto but Sullivan's music was not ready until the November. This meant that there would be a last minute panic, as it was literally days before first night. Gilbert chose the cast and selected actors that could sing and be trained to play the parts, rather than using established professionals.

He chose George Grossmith for the part of the sorcerer. He had been a former press reporter and pianist. Mrs Howard Paul was selected to play Lady Sangazur; she ran her own touring company and was an actress with excellent connections and influence. Many of the other members of the cast were students or provincial performers. A large number of the members of the chorus were drawn from the Royal Academy of Music.

D'Oyly Carte leased Opéra Comique, a small theatre just off the Strand. *The Sorcerer* would open on November 17 1877 and would run for 178 performances.

The Sorcerer

Grossmith would become a huge star; it was an inspired choice. Whilst it was not the best of Gilbert and Sullivan's work, undoubtedly the role of John Wellington Wells, played by Grossmith, was one of their best comic characters. In fact *The Sorcerer* became something of a blueprint for Gilbert and Sullivan works of the future. For the first time Gilbert and Sullivan had a completely free hand; they controlled casting, rehearsal and production. Gilbert later said:

> "To few authors indeed has such absolute control been accorded, and it is to that absolute control that I attribute a large measure of the success that those pieces achieved."

The Sorcerer was very English, from the music to the setting, and from the characters to the costumes. It did extremely well, but the theatre was not always completely full. *The Sorcerer* was covering its expenses, but it was soon clear that another opera would be needed. *The Times* reviewed the opening night:

> "Messrs. W. S. Gilbert and Arthur Sullivan have once again combined their efforts with the happiest result. *The Sorcerer*, produced at the Opéra Comique on Saturday night before an

audience that crowded the theatre in every part, achieved a genuine success, and, moreover, a success in every respect deserved. Though styled by the authors 'comic opera', the chief incident partaking of the mock-supernatural brings it within the limits of extravaganza. It is, however, extravaganza of the best, set forth in Mr. Gilbert's raciest manner, full of genial humour and such droll fancies as come to him so readily, but with little or no trace of the cynical sarcasm with which he is occasionally charged. The plot hangs upon a 'philtre', or elixir, those who taste of which become enamoured instantaneously of the first persons they happen to meet who may also have yielded to the seduction. The idea of the love potion exists from time immemorial – from *Tristan and Iseult*, the fate-struck lovers whom Wagner has resuscitated, to the *Philtre* of Auber and the *Elisir d'Amore* of Donizetti.

Mr. Gilbert's treatment of the subject, nevertheless, is quite original, the libretto finding its source in a Christmas story contributed by him some time ago to the *Graphic*. The 'Sorcerer' here, though a no less consummate charlatan to all appearance than the renowned Dulcamara, is gifted with powers not conferred by unearthly agency upon that specious quack; for while Dulcamara's elixir, innocent as the 'cattivo port-wine' of which Ronconi used to speak, could only impose upon an already love-stricken simpleton like Nemorino, that of Mr. Gilbert's hero is an unquestionably diabolic compound. This is shown in the 'incantation' required to produce it, and the lamentable fate of its promulgator, who expiates his errors at the end by a descent through sulphurous fire to the nether regions. 'Mr. John Wellington Wells, of the firm of J. W. Wells and Co., Family Sorcerers', is all the more odd and diverting from the fact of his being costumed in the garb of a respectable tradesman of the present time – in which, it may be remarked, the action of the opera is fixed. His peculiar 'philtre', when brought into use, sets the entire population of a village by the ears.

To explain how this occurs it is necessary to glance briefly at the chief *dramatis personæ*. These are Sir Marmaduke Pointdextre (Mr. R. Temple), whose son, Alexis, of the Grenadier Guards (Mr. Bentham), is about to wed Aline (Miss Alice May), daughter of Lady Sangazure (Mrs. Howard Paul); Dr. Daly (Mr. Rutland

Barrington), vicar of Ploverleigh, the village referred to; Mrs. Partlet (Miss Everard), a pew-opener whose young daughter Constance (Miss Giulia Warwick), before the 'philtre' comes into question, unaccountably entertains a strong affection for the Vicar, who, though old enough to be her grandfather, is unconscious of her preference; a notary (Mr. Clifton), who draws up the wedding contract for Alexis and his bride; and Mr. Wellington Wells himself (Mr. George Grossmith), the necromantically mysterious cause of the imbroglio.

In Act 1 the tenantry are assembled in the gardens of Sir Marmaduke's house to celebrate the approaching affiance. Aline and Alexis are sensitive young people, but the lady is more absolutely trusting than her future spouse, in whom she entertains unbounded confidence. Alexis has read something about a 'patent oxy-hydrogen love-at-first-sight philtre' advertised by Wells and Co., of St. Mary Axe, and not only desires to make certain of Aline's enduring affection, by trying it upon her, but, 'from philanthropic motives' to distribute it among the villagers. Accordingly he summons Mr. Wells, orders a sufficient quantity of the liquid for his purpose, and has it mixed with the tea which is to form part of the banquet prepared for the festive occasion. The Vicar makes the tea for his parishioners, who all drink of it, though the tender inducements of Alexis have not prevailed upon Aline to join them. 'Half an hour' is supposed to be the interval between the first and the second acts, and this half hour has successfully accomplished its work before the curtain rises upon Act 2.

First we find Constance, Mrs. Partlet's daughter, transferring her affections from the Vicar to the Notary; then we learn from the Vicar that the inhabitants of Ploverleigh have come to his residence in a body, imploring him, couple after couple, to fasten them in the bonds of matrimony, old people with young, and *vice versa* – 'not a match among them,' remarks the inexorable Aline, 'that the hollow world would consider well-advised.' Even old Sir Marmaduke Pointdextre has made proposals to, and been accepted by, Mrs. Partlet, the venerable pew-opener; and, awful to contemplate, the proud and stately Lady Sangazure makes a dead set at Mr. Wells, the sorcerer, he not having drunk of his own philtre, being anything rather than fascinated. Worst of all, Aline, beginning herself to be nervous about the possible constancy of Alexis, swallows some of the fatal nostrum, and as, with slow steps and in tristful mood, she retires to tell her lover how she has obeyed his wish, encounters Dr. Daly, and straightway becomes enamoured of the Vicar, who, under the same influence, responds without hesitation. The nature of the kind old gentleman, however, revolting against this unhoped-for position, restores Aline to her lover, the disappearance of the sorcerer, in the exceptional circumstances alluded to, undoing the spell which the administration of his 'philtre' had exercised. The newly formed attachments are then immediately exchanged for the old loves; and the curtain falls on a general rejoicing, in anticipation of a fresh wedding feast, at which, though tea is again to be the chief beverage, it will be tea without 'elixir'.

Strange as this plot may be pronounced, so cleverly is it developed that, the impossible world through which the author conducts his spectator once admitted, it appears consistent enough – the only inexplicable feature being the sudden means of its unravelment. Supernatural incidents, however, involve supernatural conclusions; and it might be hard to suggest to Mr. Gilbert another way of extricating his characters from the difficulty under which he has placed them.

There are so many good things in the music of Mr. Sullivan that to dwell upon them *seriatim* would occupy far more space than is now available. A line or two must, therefore, suffice for the moment. Above all, the music is spontaneous, appearing invariably to spring out of the dramatic situations, as though it was their natural concomitant. It is also distinguished by marked character and skilfully varied in accordance with the nature of the incidents its composer has had to illustrate; while, as essentially comic as the story and dialogue themselves, and fitting both to admiration, it is everywhere tuneful, and comprises not a few concerted pieces of the highest expressive merit, showing also in their construction and working out (as might be expected from Mr. Sullivan) the hand of a practised master. Those who look for such sallies of humorous musical definition as are to be met with in *Cox and Box*, the

Contrabandista, and *Trial by Jury*, will not be disappointed, there being several examples which may rank with anything the composer has written in this style. *The Sorcerer* contains fewer attempts as what may, with submission, be termed 'burlesques' upon favourite existing models than any one of its precursors. It aims, indeed, in the greater number of instances at a higher mark, seldom failing to reach it.

The orchestra, according to Mr. Sullivan's usual method of treating such subjects, takes a conspicuous part in the humorous delineation of personages and incidents, and as he is thoroughly acquainted with every resource of that important element in operatic music, it need scarcely be added that it is invariably used with pointed and well-considered effect. Since, however, there is more to be said about the music of this very entertaining production, the foregoing general observations will for the present answer all purposes. Enough that by this new effort Mr. Sullivan has certainly not deteriorated from, but, on the contrary, added to his well-earned repute.

A more careful first performance of a new work of its kind has rarely been witnessed. The orchestra and chorus were excellent, and quite strong enough for the size of the theatre – the former numbering nearly 30, the latter upwards of 40. The leading singers, whose names are given above, were also thoroughly efficient, every one of them, doing all that was practicable to insure an effective 'ensemble' and succeeding in proportion. To them, also, some words of acknowledgement will be due on returning to consideration of the music. Mr. Sullivan directed the performance, and, with Mr. Gilbert, was called before the lamps at the conclusion, amid applause the genuine nature of which could never once have been mistaken. In short, the audience had been diverted from the rise of the curtain to the fall, and the laughter was incessant.

The Sorcerer was preceded by Mr. Alfred Cellier's one-act operetta, *Dora's Dream* (libretto by Mr. Arthur Cecil), with Miss Giulia Warwick and Mr. R. Temple as Fred Fencourt and Dora Leslie. This pleasant and sparkling *bagatelle* at once put the house in good humour."

The Sorcerer Cast and Synopsis

Sir Marmaduke Pointdexter	Richard Temple
Alexis (his son)	George Bentham
Dr Daly (the rector)	Rutland Barrington
Notary	Fred Clifton
John Wellington Wells	George Grossmith
Lady Sangazure	Mrs Howard Paul
Aline (her daughter)	Alice May
Mrs Partlett (Pew Opener)	Helen Everard
Constance (her daughter)	Guilia Warwick
Chorus of villagers	

Act I

Alexis, a Grenadier Guard, is celebrating the announcement of his marriage to Aline and is enjoying a banquet on the lawn of their family mansion. Ploverleigh villagers have also been invited. Amongst them is Mrs Partlett and her daughter Constance. Constance loves the village rector, Dr Daly. He is unreceptive to Mrs Partlett's subtle hints. Aline arrives with Lady Sangazure and the latter was a childhood sweetheart of Marmaduke. Alexis wants everyone to share his good fortune and he contacts a London-based sorcerer about love potions. The sorcerer, John Wellington Wells, arrives and provides him with a potion that works on unmarried people. Dr Daly brews up the tea with the potion and those that drink it fall asleep.

Act II

The sleepers will awake at midnight and anyone that is unmarried will fall in love with the first person that they see. Constance falls in love with the elderly, deaf notary and once everyone has paired off only Dr Daly does not have a partner. Alexis wants him and Aline to take the potion to ensure that they remain in love forever, but Aline is angry. Their argument is interrupted by Dr Daly, who cannot understand why everybody wants to get married. Alexis, to his horror, sees that his father has partnered up with Mrs Partlett. Lady Sangazure has fallen for the sorcerer. Aline decides to take the potion and tries to find Alexis, but instead bumps into Dr Daly and falls in love with him. Alexis is furious and corners the sorcerer and orders him to reverse the spell. The only

A poster advertising The Sorcerer, HMS Pinafore *and* Trial by Jury *performed by the Saville English Opera Company in around 1879.* From the Library of Congress collection.

way that this can be achieved is for either Alexis or the sorcerer to die. The sorcerer is the most obvious candidate and he disappears in smoke and fire, cancelling the effects of the potion and everyone returns to normal. Alexis has Aline, Sir Marmaduke has Lady Sangazure, Constance has Dr Daly and the notary has Mrs Partlett.

Typecasting

The group of actors that had been brought together by Gilbert and Sullivan for *The Sorcerer* were to find familiar roles in future operas. George Grossmith would go on to play Sir Joseph Porter, The Lord Chancellor, Reginald Bunthorne, Major-General Stanley, Jack Point, Robin Oakapple, Ko-Ko and King Gama, following on from his portrayal of John Wellington Wells. In fact the part of Wells had been written with Frederic Sullivan in mind.

Rutland Barrington would go on to play Captain Corcoran, Archibald Grosvenor, King Hildebrand, the Sergeant of Police, the Earl of Mountararat, Pooh-Bah, King Paramount, Ludwig, Giuseppe and Sir Despard Murgatroyd.

Soon Richard Temple and Jessie Bond would join the company in time for *HMS Pinafore*. The plots would also have a familiar pattern; from *Trial by Jury* all the way to *Princess Ida* in 1884, all were set in Victorian England. From *Princess Ida* onwards the operas were set in more exotic locations. Another emerging pattern would be the introductory scene-setting chorus. Also in many cases the chorus would marry by the end of the opera.

It seems clear that Gilbert and Sullivan knew exactly what they were doing and had established a blueprint. They allowed the principal actors to interpret their roles, but it was always Gilbert that had the final say. In most of the operas the female chorus always had bright and lively entrance tunes, whilst the male chorus usually had a military, or dignified, number. Many of the heroines had tainted characters and many of the male ones were self-centred. Perhaps this was because these male heroes were often tenors and not physically heroic-looking.

Gilbert always found room in his operas for older women and his male comic leads would always have their own, individual songs. Gilbert also introduced what became known as the ensemble of perplexity, where members of the cast sang about the problems within the plot. There was also role reversal; in *The Sorcerer* village people had fallen in love with their social superiors, in *Thespis* mortals had exchanged roles with Gods, in *The Pirates of Penzance* pirates became noblemen. There were also twists in logic; in four of the operas legal solutions were sought, including *The Grand Duke*, *Ruddigore*, *Iolanthe* and *The Mikado*. In addition there were characters changing places so that a solution could be found, in *Thespis*, *Trial by Jury*, *HMS Pinafore*, *Patience*, *The Gondoliers*, *Princess Ida*, *The Sorcerer* and *The Yeoman of the Guard*. Gilbert also incorporated social comment, cynicism and comment on Victorian standards. Parliament, ideas and institutions were not immune from his sharp wit.

Undoubtedly *The Sorcerer* proved to be a valuable pattern, providing a framework for the storylines and for the characters. At the same time, however, Sullivan moved away from his parody of other composers and began to create his own distinctive work.

HMS Pinafore

Sullivan was delighted when he received Gilbert's libretto for *HMS Pinafore*. Gilbert had sauntered around the deck of *HMS Victory* in Portsmouth on April 13, 1878. He had lunched with Lord Charles Beresford and had spent time making sketches. His diary recorded:

An 1879 New York HMS Pinafore *poster from the Library of Congress collection.*

"Went onboard *Victory* and *St Vincent*, making sketches, then pulled ashore to station."

François Cellier wrote:

"From the sketches he made onboard the *Victory* he was able to prepare a complete model of the Pinafore's deck. With the aid of this model, with varied coloured blocks to represent the principals and chorus, Gilbert, like an experienced general, worked out his plan of campaign in the retirement of his studio, and so came to the theatre ready prepared to marshal his company. The perfect state of preparedness in which *HMS Pinafore* was launched showed Gilbert to be the master-absolute of stage craft."

In fact Gilbert had built a ½-inch scale model of the stage with each entrance and exit shown. The men were represented by 3-inch high blocks and the women 2½-inch blocks. Each block was in a different colour, to show tenors, sopranos, etc. Gilbert worked out every position for each character.

Sullivan had been in France but received a message calling him back to England. Meanwhile D'Oyly Carte was rounding up all of the artists that had performed in *The Sorcerer*. Jessie Bond, who would play Hebe, was delighted when she received a telegram from D'Oyly Carte:

"It was like a trumpet call to go on the stage, to play in a company which was doing something entirely new and original in light opera! The name of Gilbert and Sullivan was already ringing through the country, I knew well what chances of advancement association with it would give to me. But – it was the Victorian era, the stage was frowned upon by the respectable, and I had been trained in the strict conditions of concert and oratorio singing. Would not such a change in my life mean social downfall, and would not my parents think I had gone to perdition? I dared not tell them of Carte's offer, I knew too well beforehand how strong their objections would be. But in my eyes the prospect was too dazzling; I could not turn away from it. I made some excuse about a pressing engagement in London, packed in hot haste, and caught the first possible train. At 11 o'clock on the appointed morning I was in Mr D'Oyly Carte's office. He offered me an engagement in his company, and without hesitation I signed a contract for three years, at the princely salary – for me – of three pounds a week."

The opening night for *HMS Pinafore* was May 25, 1878. Sir George Douglas witnessed the first performance:

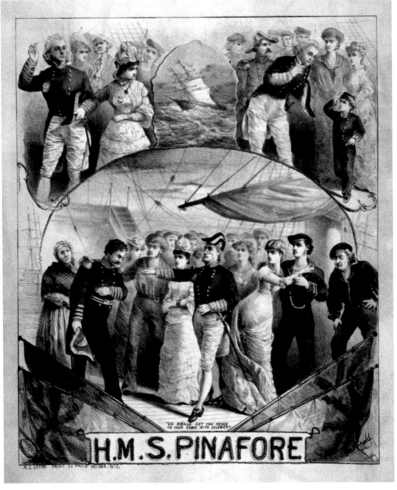

A poster for one of the US productions of HMS Pinafore, *almost certainly one of the pirate versions. It is dated around 1879 and part of the US Library of Congress Collection.*

"There was no room for fault-finding whether in music, play, or acting. One heard that night for the first time words and airs that have remained with one ever since, and that straight way became a part of the national inheritance."

Gilbert in particular was extremely stressed about the whole lead up to the opening night. It was one of his foibles that he would not watch first night, but would roam the streets. On May 25 he came in and out of the theatre four times. He had been working on rewrites until the early hours of the morning and just three weeks before the first performance he was still revising it. The rehearsals were incredibly intensive and on the day before first night he spent the whole day and half the night in the theatre. He was up again the following morning to supervise the last minute touches.

In fact *HMS Pinafore* could not have opened at a worse time. It was incredibly hot in London and audiences found sitting in theatres too uncomfortable. Within a few days box office receipts began to fall and by July they had dropped to less than £40 a night. It was touch and go as to whether the production would be pulled. The cast agreed to a 30 per cent wage cut and a selection of tunes from the show were played at the promenade concerts at the Covent Garden Theatre; this helped to stimulate ticket sales. In double quick time D'Oyly Carte organised two touring companies to take the show across the country.

The Times reviewed the opening night as follows:

"On Saturday night *H.M.S. Pinafore*, a new 'original nautical comic opera', the joint production of Mr. W. G. Gilbert (sic) and Mr. Arthur Sullivan, saw the light of the stage. Like its predecessor from the same source, *The Sorcerer*, it bids fair to open a new and successful epoch in the history of the pretty theatre in the Strand, where English opera under the auspices of Mr. D'Oyly Carte has found a congenial home. We apply the words 'English opera' by some stretch of courtesy, for as yet the attempt at the establishment of a national musical stage is of a somewhat modest kind. But the fact ought to be acknowledged that here we have a libretto by an English dramatist and music by an English composer; the former witty and amusing, without a shadow of the more or less veiled improprieties characteristic of French importations; and the latter melodious and admirably constructed without the aid of German or Italian models.

Mr. Gilbert's plot, if such it can be called, is of the simplest description. The scene is laid on board Her Majesty's Ship Pinafore, Captain Corcoran, commander Captain and crew are on cordial terms with each other, and express their mutual goodwill in the most energetic and, at the same time, melodious manner. Readers of the 'Bab Ballads' will at once recognize 'worthy Captain Reece' as the original of the philanthropic naval officer. In one respect only does the dramatized captain differ from his prototype. He shares the prejudices of his caste on the subject of matrimonial alliances. His daughter Josephine loves a humble sailor, but her father insists upon her giving her hand to the Right Hon. Sir Joseph Porter, First Lord of the Admiralty. The arrival of this worthy, who, it appears, is always accompanied by an admiring crowd of female relatives, is duly announced by a barcarole, and a responsive chorus of sailors.

The mental attitude of Sir Joseph is, if possible, still more remarkable than that of Captain Corcoran. The reticence of office is strange to his soul, and immediately on his arrival he begins to tell the assembled crew of his antecedents, including his humble calling as office boy to an attorney and his gradual rise through the stages of junior clerkship and partnership to his present exalted position. As regards indifference to social prejudices he even exceeds Captain Corcoran, and insists, for example, that to every word of command addressed to the humblest cabin boy a polite 'If you please' should be added. We have dwelt upon these whimsicalities of characterization at some length because it is in them that the interest of the libretto entirely centres.

The story may be told in the fewest words. A lady, Little Buttercup by name, and a Portsmouth 'bumboat woman' by calling, who in her youth has practised baby farming, unburdens her conscience to the effect that she has exchanged in their cradles Captain Corcoran and Ralph Rackstraw, his daughter's wooer; whereat Sir Joseph withdraws his suit and Josephine becomes the prize of the lucky sailor, who has found a fortune and a bride at the same moment. Other characters of the play are the precipitately wedded, and the curtain drops. This may seem an easy way of constructing a drama. But with Mr. Gilbert a plot is seldom more than a lay figure which he delights in dressing in the fantastic garb of his wit and imagination. In the present instance, also, his dialogue sparkles with the most curious *concetti*, and vagaries of expression, and while listening to these we hardly become conscious of the absence of any kind of human interest.

The audience, therefore, have little reason to complain of Mr. Gilbert. But the musician has. His true field of action is after all genuine emotion; witticisms and *jeux-de-mots* are of little avail to him. The manner in which Mr. Sullivan accepts the difficult position thus prepared for him by his collaborator is worthy of the highest commendation. Whenever he finds that Mr. Gilbert's humour cannot be aided by musical means he lets well alone and retires to modest recitative. On the other hand, he loses no opportunity of emphasizing comic points or indicating hidden irony by a slight touch of exaggeration. A very unsophisticated audience might accept, for instance, Ralph's ballad, 'A maiden fair to see' as the real sentiment of which it is an admirable caricature, or mistake that admirable specimen of the 'mock-heroic', 'I am an Englishman, behold me' for genuine patriotic bluster. The terrific *roulade* accompanying the bold announcement of the gallant boatswain deserves especial praise. That the music of so melodious a writer as Mr. Sullivan is full of charming tunes, it is hardly necessary to add. The madrigal in the first act, 'The Nightingale' and Josephine's ballad, 'Sorry her lot who loves too well' are certain to be hailed with welcome in the drawing-room, where they will, perhaps, be more in their place than in the opera. Much superior to these is the truly pathetic snatch of melody belonging to an 'aside' in the love duet between Ralph and Josephine and occurring also in the overture.

The most important *ensemble* is the *finale* of the first act, where Mr. Sullivan successfully grapples with the difficult problem of grouping his characters according to the nature of their utterances without disturbing the harmony of the whole. Much less satisfactory is the finale of the second act, largely made up of the tunes previously used, and not sufficiently welded together. This

George Grossmith as Sir Joseph Porter and Jessie Bond as Hebe in HMS Pinafore.

piece and the overture betray unmistakable signs of hurry, which Mr. Sullivan might remove with a little trouble. Among the concerted pieces of the second act a short but admirably written octet and a duet between Captain Corcoran and Dick Deadeye, the villain of the piece, deserve to be mentioned, the latter piece being especially remarkable for a charming orchestral *ritornel.*

The performance of the work was in many respects excellent. Few theatres can boast such a trio of genuine humorists as are (Sir Joseph Porter), Mr. Rutland Barrington (the philanthropic captain), and Miss Everard (Little Buttercup). The vocal achievements of these artists are not of the highest order, but their *parlato* style does full justice to the humorous sallies of Mr. Gilbert. Mr. Power (Ralph Rackstraw) and Miss Emma Howson (Josephine) were on the other hand a sweet-voiced pair of lovers. The gentleman is in possession of a sympathetic although not very powerful tenor voice, which he uses to good advantage, although on the first night his intonation was a little uncertain. Miss Howson, as far as we are aware a novice on the stage, is a singer of decided promise. Her voice is a light soprano of an agreeable quality, and her singing betrays musical intelligence and dramatic instinct.

Chorus and orchestra acquitted themselves of their by no means easy task in a very creditable manner, and the performance – conducted on the first night by the composer himself – was received by a crowded audience with every sign of satisfaction. While recording this decided success of Mr. Sullivan's new work we cannot suppress a word of regret that the composer on whom before all others the chances of a national school of music depend should confine himself, or be confined by circumstances, to a class of production which, however attractive, is hardly worthy of the efforts of an accomplished and serious artist."

HMS Pinafore Cast and Synopsis

The Right Honourable Sir Joseph Porter, KCB	George Grossmith
Captain Corcoran	Rutland Barrington
Ralph Rackstraw	George Power
Dick Deadeye	Richard Temple
Bill Bobstay	Fred Clifton
Bob Becket	Mr Dymott
Tom Tucker	Master Fitzaltamont
Sergeant of Marines	Mr Talbot
Josephine	Emma Howson
Hebe	Jessie Bond
Little Buttercup	Helen Everard

Act I

The action opens on the deck of HMS Pinafore. The sailors are buying items from Little Buttercup, who is in a boat alongside their ship. Two characters, Dick Deadeye and Ralph Rackstraw, appear and Ralph

A poster for HMS Pinafore, *undated but possibly 1876. From the Library of Congress collection.*

An original US poster for HMS Pinafore. From the Library of Congress collection.

admits that he is in love with the captain's daughter. The captain welcomes the crew and he tells Buttercup that his daughter, Josephine, is much admired by the First Lord of the Admiralty, Sir Joseph Porter. Porter wants to marry her, but Josephine is not keen. Josephine tells her father that she is in love with a sailor. Sir Joseph arrives with his family entourage and he gives the crew new songs that will be sung by the Royal Navy. They then sing them and Ralph is left alone with Josephine. She is obviously interested, but she turns him away. Ralph announces that he will commit suicide and readies a pistol. In the nick of time Josephine admits that she does love Ralph. The couple decide to elope that night.

Act II

This opens with Captain Corcoran singing of his worries about his daughter and Buttercup joins him. She admits that she is a fortune teller and that the captain should prepare himself for a major life change. Sir Joseph is worried that Josephine is not interested in him, but her father reassures him that it is just his high rank. Dick Deadeye tells the captain about the planned elopement and he intercedes just as the couple are about to leave. Ralph tells the captain how much he loves Josephine. Sir Joseph appears and ushers the captain away, clapping Ralph in irons. Buttercup now tells them that she looked after Ralph and the captain when they were children and that she mixed them up, so Ralph should be the captain and the captain a seaman. The two men re-emerge on deck in one another's clothes. Ralph can now marry Josephine. The captain asks Buttercup to marry him and Sir Joseph is comforted by his first cousin, Hebe.

HMS Pinafore was lurching toward disaster. Whilst Gilbert and Sullivan and D'Oyly Carte retained their faith in the production, the other directors were less optimistic. On July 31, 1879, during the 374th performance, and with the lease of the theatre coming to an end, a group of men appeared, with instructions from the other directors to remove the scenery and move it to another theatre, where they would launch a revival. Horse drawn removal vans had been arranged and a rival company was actually being formed at the Imperial Theatre in Westminster. It then moved to the Olympic and finally to the Standard, in Shoreditch.

D'Oyly Carte was in the United States at the time. For the time being Gilbert took on men with sandwich boards to walk the streets, telling the public where the authorised performance was being held. Gilbert and Sullivan and D'Oyly Carte took the matter to court and won. By the time this happened the rival company had gone bankrupt and the three men not only failed to receive any damages but also had to pay their own costs.

The rival directors were paid off and a new company was set up on August 4, 1879, known as Mr D'Oyly Carte's Opera Company. The three men each put £1,000 into the new company. The deal was that Gilbert and Sullivan would receive a wage of 4 guineas each for every performance and D'Oyly Carte would be paid £15 per week.

A young woman from the cast of HMS Pinafore *posed against a painted backdrop and believed to have been taken around 1879.* From the Library of Congress collection.

A children's version of *HMS Pinafore* ran from December 1879 until March 1880, with the music rearranged for younger voices. Meanwhile *HMS Pinafore* had crossed the Atlantic and at one time there were six different productions in Philadelphia and no less than eight in New York. This culminated in no less than 50 different companies performing the opera across the United States. These were all pirate performances and many of them were semi-amateur. The first British amateur production was performed at the Kingston-upon-Thames Drill Hall in April 1879.

D'Oyly Carte did his best to try to stop these unauthorised American productions by organising his own. They took a cast to the United States and the first authorised performance launched at the Fifth Avenue

A black of white lithograph from New York, dated 1879, for W S Gilbert's burlesque comedy Engaged. *From the Library of Congress collection.*

Theatre in New York at the beginning of December 1879. Gilbert himself appeared in the chorus. It is believed that this was the only time that Gilbert ever appeared on stage on a first night in one of his own operas. It was a tremendous hit and the Americans loved the blend of comedy and tragedy.

The most significant part of this confusing time was the establishment of the partnership between the three men. They would equally share profits after all expenses but this arrangement would come back to bite them 12 years later.

It was whilst Gilbert and Sullivan were in New York, sorting out the official version of *HMS Pinafore* that secret rehearsals began for their next opera. They had taken draft versions of *The Pirates of Penzance* across the Atlantic with them. Their idea was a solid one; if they could open in New York they could obtain copyright protection and stop all of

A woman from the cast of Gilbert and Sullivan's HMS Pinafore *taken in 1879.* From the Library of Congress collection.

the pirate productions from taking place. Ensconced in a hotel in Manhattan Sullivan completed the score, but there had been a problem, as the draft of the first act had been left back in London and it had to be written again from memory.

Sullivan completed the score at seven in the morning on December 28; the dress rehearsal was due to take place on December 29 and the opening night was the 31st. The rehearsal took place at the Fifth Avenue Theatre under extremely tight security. Originally, *The Pirates of Penzance* was to be called *The Robbers*. The partners had also taken the precaution of launching a very low key performance a day before the grand opening in New York. So it was that at the Royal Bijou Theatre in Paignton, Devon, a matinee performance was put on in front of an audience of 50 people by one of the D'Oyly Carte touring companies on December 30. The touring company had only had one dress rehearsal, straight after a performance of *HMS Pinafore*. They also had only a portion of the music; they had no proper costumes and they sang with their sheet music in front of them.

The New York opening took place on New Year's Eve and Sullivan conducted. The lead up to the production had also had other problems, as Sullivan himself explained:

"We had been rehearsing *The Pirates* and it was but two or three days before the performance that the whole band went on strike. They explained that the music was not ordinary operetta music, but more like grand opera. Perhaps it is necessary to explain that their method is to charge according to a scale, so much per week for entr'acte music, with an ascending scale for operetta, and so on. Had they made their complaint earlier no doubt matters could have been arranged satisfactorily, but their going on strike for higher salaries at the very last moment in this way appealed to me as being a very mean thing to do. Under the circumstances I felt there was nothing for it but to grapple as best I could with the emergency. I called the band together and told them that I was much flattered by the compliment they had paid my music, but declined to submit to their demands. I went on to say that the concerts at Covent Garden, which I conducted, had just been concluded, and the orchestra there, which was the finest in England, had very little to do before the opera season began, and that I was certain that, on receiving a cable to that effect, they would come over to America to oblige me for little more than their expenses. In the meantime I told them I should go on with the opera, playing the pianoforte myself, and with my friend Mr Alfred Cellier at the harmonium, and that when the Covent Garden orchestra did come, we should have a very much finer band than we could get in New York. Then I went to my friend, the manager of the *New York Herald*, and asked him to write an article in the shape of an interview with me on the subject, which he did, and I launched out freely with my opinions. The upshot of it all was that the band gave in, and everything went along smoothly. Of course, the idea of getting the Covent Garden band over was hardly less absurd than the ludicrous idea of using the pianoforte and harmonium in a big theatre, but, fortunately, public opinion was with me, and my one game of bluff was successful."

Piracy was still a major problem and Gilbert and Sullivan sent out four different companies to tour around America. They put on shows at Boston, Buffalo, Chicago, Lewisville, Memphis, New Orleans, Newark and Philadelphia. As an extra precautionary measure all of the manuscripts were collected up after each performance and locked away in a safe. Pirate printers even tried to send musicians into the theatres to copy out the music; most of the time they had to try to memorise the music in order to present it.

With *The Pirates of Penzance* doing amazing business in America, Gilbert and Sullivan sailed home for England in March 1880.

The Pirates of Penzance

The Pirates of Penzance opened in London on April 3, 1880. It was its third first night performance and it ran at the Opéra Comique for 363 performances. *The Times* review of the first night of the original London production stated:

"When the curtain rises we see the far-famed Pirates of Penzance reposing in picturesque groups, the scene being a rocky shore on the coast of Cornwall. They are celebrating the coming of age of Frederic, one of the bravest members of their band, who alone is sad among the merry. The cause of his sadness is sufficiently explained by the ballad of Ruth, the nursery-maid, to whose care young Frederic had been left by his father:–

'I was a stupid nursery-maid, on breakers always steering,

And I did not catch the word aright through being hard of hearing;

Mistaking my instructions, which within my mind did gyrate,

I took and bound this promising lad apprentice to a pirate.

A sad mistake it was to make, and doom him to a vile lot,

I bound him to a pirate – you – instead of to a pilot.'

This is, indeed, a slender peg to support even the thinnest web of a story, slenderer even than the mistake which in the Pinafore

The original theatrical poster for the 1880 US production of The Pirates of Penzance. *Theatrical poster collection of the Library of Congress.*

made Little Buttercup – by the way, the exact prototype of Ruth – 'mix those children up, and not a creature knew it.' To return to the Pirates of Penzance, it must be owned that they follow their criminal calling in a very humane and gentlemanly spirit. They, for example, never attack a weaker party than themselves, and, moreover, make a point of never molesting an orphan. This latter circumstance has become generally known, and is taken advantage of by the victims of the bold pirates. 'The last three ships we took,' they complain, 'proved to be manned entirely by orphans, and so we had to let them go.'

But in spite of these redeeming features Frederic declares himself disgusted with the society he has been compelled to keep. Being a 'slave of duty' he has felt bound to further the ends of the pirates while his apprenticeship continued; but the same sense of duty, he confesses freely, compels him 'to devote himself heart and soul to their extermination now that he is out of his indentures.' Acting on the same strict principle, he is on the point of giving his hand to the middle-aged Ruth, when their interview is interrupted by the voices of young ladies, who are presently seen approaching. Frederic, who had never seen a young maiden in his life, at once perceives the falsehood of his nurse, who had represented herself to him as the ideal of womanhood, and, feeling once more at liberty, proposes to one and several of the maidens – four-and-twenty in number – who turn out to be sisters. They all refuse him except the romantically-minded Mabel, who at first sight falls in love with the picturesque ex-pirate. In the meantime the pirates have returned to the scene, and, surrounding the maidens, propose in their turn to be as they express it:

'Conjugally matrimonified
By a Doctor of Divinity
Who is located in this vicinity.'

This interesting meeting is interrupted by the arrival of Major-General Stanley. Major-General Stanley is the alter ego of the First Lord of the Admiralty in the Pinafore. Like that functionary, he immediately sets forth his qualifications for his high office in a song, which in sentiment is the counterpart of the popular ballad of 'the Ruler of the Queen's Navie' (sic) while in the matter of impossible rhymes it might have excited the envy of the author of 'Hudibras' himself.

The place of the famous 'sisters and cousins and aunts' is taken in the present instance by the 24 daughters of Major-General Stanley already introduced to the reader. The difficulties of the situation are met by the ready wit of the aged warrior, who on proclaiming himself a 'lonely orphan boy' is allowed by the tender-hearted pirates to depart in peace, together with his daughters and Frederic.

The latter, in the second act, is bent upon obeying the dictates of duty by exterminating his former comrades, and for that purpose has surrounded himself with a set of policemen, about as bold and as musical as their colleagues, the two gendarmes in Offenbach's Genevieve of Brabant. But this noble endeavour is frustrated by a fresh discovery of a very extraordinary character. His apprenticeship, it appears, was stipulated to last until his 21st birthday, and that birthday falling on the 29th of February, he is accordingly still tied to the pirates for an unlimited number of years. Having become a pirate again, he feels in duty bound to disclose the falsehood of the General as to his being an orphan. This breach of faith the fierce rovers of the sea determine to revenge in the most ruthless manner. They easily vanquish the policemen sent out to capture them, and are on the point of committing the gallant soldier to death when a last appeal 'to yield in Queen Victoria's name' recalls them to their duty. After this the denouement is short and satisfactory. Ruth exclaims, referring to the pirates, –

'They are no members of the common throng,
They are all noblemen who have gone wrong.'

'What all noblemen?' ask the policemen and girls. 'Well, nearly all,' is the answer, in palpable allusion to the proverbial 'hardly ever' of the Pinafore. We need not add that the wooing of members of the House of Peers is not rejected by General Stanley and his daughters, 'all of whom' it is generally admitted, 'are beauties'.

Such a story, lighted up with the incessant fireworks of Mr. Gilbert's wit, contains all the elements of popularity, and on its own peculiar grounds little fault can be found with it from a literary point of view. But it is different when we regard it as the basis of musical construction, as a libretto. Music is fully able to deal with broadly comic phases of human life. Such a character as say, Figaro, in the scores of Rossini and of Mozart, stands forth with a graphic distinctness unattainable by words alone. But Mr. Gilbert's characters are not comic in themselves, but only in reference to other characters chiefly of the operatic type, whose exaggerated attitude and parlance they mimic. He writes not, in fact, comedies but parodies, and music has accordingly to follow him to the sphere of all others most uncongenial to it – the mock-heroic. The skill and ingenuity evinced by Mr. Sullivan in such disadvantageous circumstances cannot be sufficiently admired. His tunes are always fresh and lively, and the few opportunities of genuine sentimental utterance offered to him are turned to excellent account. One such opportunity – the leave-taking of Frederic and Mabel in the second act – has originated a sweetly melodious madrigal ('Oh leave me not'), another has called forth Mabel's song in the first act, 'Poor wandering one.' Certain passages in the first duet between Frederic and Ruth and elsewhere, where the composer becomes serious in spite of himself, make one regret what might have been, or, perhaps, might still be if Mr. Sullivan would attempt a genuine dramatic effort. As a piece of very graceful concerted writing we may mention the discreet chatter of the girls 'about the weather' accompanying in an undertone the amorous discourse of Frederic and Mabel. More broadly comic pieces, such as the pirates' chorus and the song of the policeman – the latter received with a perfect storm of applause – will be welcome food for street organs and popular minstrels. Taken as a whole, however, the music to the Pirates of Penzance did not seem quite equal to that of the Pinafore, certainly not to that of The Sorcerer, in our opinion the masterpiece of its joint authors.

The question of popular success is of course quite different from artistic merit. On the first night the satisfaction of the crowded audience was boundless, culminating in the call before the curtain of the performers (including the four-and-twenty maidens) and the authors. Of the rendering we can speak in brief and highly favourable terms. The mis-en-scène did great credit to the establishment over which Mr. D'Oyly Carte presides, and the admirable singing of the chorus testified to careful and conscientious rehearsing under the composer's direction. The comic gravity of Mr. George Grossmith's General Stanley may be imagined by those who have seen that excellent artist as Sir Joseph Porter, K.C.B., in the Pinafore. Mr. Barrington was absolutely sublime in the small but by no means unimportant part of Sergeant of Police, and Mr. Power's sympathetic tenor voice was heard to great advantage in the sentimental music allotted to the dutiful Frederic. Mr. R. Temple, as the Pirate King, was as truculent as could well be desired. Miss Marian Hood (Mabel) is in possession of a fine soprano voice of considerable compass, which, but for her habit of straining it, would be very sympathetic. The bravura passages with which Mr. Sullivan has adorned the part were attacked with considerable courage and success, and the pretty madrigal already referred to was given with exquisite feeling. Further careful study may make an excellent singer of Miss Hood. Miss Cross, who owing to Miss Everard's indisposition took the part of Ruth at very short notice, acquitted herself most creditably. A few slips of memory were fully accounted for in the circumstances."

Character	Paignton	New York	London
Major-General Stanley	Richard Mansfield	J H Ryley	George Grossmith
The Pirate King	Frederick Federici	Signor Brocolini	Richard Temple
Frederick	Llewellyn Cadwaladr	Hugh Talbot	George Power
Samuel	G J Lackner	Furneaux Cook	George Temple
James	John le Hay		
Sergeant of Police	Fred Billington	Fred Clifton	Rutland Barrington
Mabel	Emilie Petrelli	Blanche Roosevelt	Marion Hood
Edith	Marian May	Rosina Brandram	Julia Gwynne
Isabel	Kate Neville	Jessie Bond	Lilian la Rue
Kate	Lena Monmouth	Billie Barlow	Neva Bond
Ruth	Fanny Harrison	Alice Barnett	Emily Cross

The Pirates of Penzance Cast and Synopsis

Act I

The pirates of Penzance have congregated to celebrate Frederick's coming of age. Frederick became a pirate apprentice by mistake when his nursery maid, Ruth, mistook instructions to apprentice the boy as a pirate instead of a pilot. To look after the boy she stayed on with the pirates. Frederick is pleased to be released from his life of piracy and he intends to wipe them all out. They are very unsuccessful pirates and often too

An 1880 print of a poster published in New York for The Pirates of Penzance. *From the Library of Congress collection.*

timid. The pirates leave Frederick and Ruth in a cove. Ruth tries to proposition Frederick, but this is interrupted when some young girls arrive. Frederick turns Ruth down and hides but he shows himself as the girls begin to undress to swim. One of the girls, Mabel, takes pity on Frederick and he warns them about the pirates. But it is too late and the pirates propose a mass marriage. Suddenly Major-General Stanley arrives. He is the girls' father and very angry. As the pirates are about to set upon Stanley he tells them that he is an orphan. They take pity on him and return his daughters.

Act II

Stanley is remorseful at the lies that he has told and his purchase of a title and a castle. Frederick gets together an expedition to attack the pirates; it is an ill-suited and ill-equipped group. Frederick is left alone and the Pirate King and Ruth arrive. They tell him that he was born on February 29, which means that he is only just over the age of five and not twenty one, so according to the apprenticeship he must return to them until his twenty first birthday. Frederick admits that Stanley told them lies and the Pirate King determines to attack his castle. The police posse tries to arrest the pirates but they are beaten off. The Sergeant of Police orders the pirates to surrender in the name of the Queen, which they do. Ruth tells the pirates that they are all really noblemen. Stanley tells them to take on their responsibilities and gives his permission for them to marry his daughters.

Whilst their new opera was doing great business in London, Sullivan travelled north to conduct his new composition, *The Martyr of Antioch*. He was widely praised for the work and his conducting skills and there were record attendances and profits for the festival in Leeds. Gilbert had reworked H. H. Milman's poem into a suitable verse for the piece.

The Pirates of Penzance was the first of the operas in which there was a three-way split between Gilbert and Sullivan and D'Oyly Carte, although even at this stage it was apparent that Sullivan received considerably more adulation than Gilbert. When they had been working together in America they saw far much more of one another than ever before. Normally their contact was by mail.

A prosperous year was coming to an end, but this was just the beginning of the golden period of partnership between Gilbert and Sullivan.

Chapter 4

The Savoy Theatre

Whilst Gilbert and Sullivan's next opera, *Patience*, opened at the Opera Comique on April 23, 1881, the year was to see the opening of the Savoy Theatre and *Patience* would be moved to the new theatre on October 10. The Prince of Wales attended the opening.

HMS Pinafore had featured discipline as the principle target of satire. Duty had been targeted in *Pirates of Penzance* but this time Gilbert would choose affectation. Gilbert had wanted to write about aesthetics and had planned to write about a pair of curates who were attracted to parishioners. But he was worried about upsetting the church. His plan had been a satire of Anglo-Catholics in the Church of England but he held back and rewrote the story so it would feature a female chorus who were in love with a poet. In fact the curtain rises with some 20 lovesick maidens, all suitably draped, and in the courtyard of Castle Munthorne. They wear pastel coloured dresses and even their attitudes satirise the then popular ways of behaviour and dress of young women.

Gilbert bought the fabrics at Liberty's, which specialised in precisely the kind of aesthetic products and decor that he was targeting. Gilbert wanted to satirise not just the trendy, literary types, but also the broader movement, including people like Oscar Wilde. In the story three Dragoon officers dispense with their uniforms and dress up like aesthetes to woe the lovesick women.

This was a highbrow comedy of manners and quite a risk. Reginald Bunthorne, the poet in the story, is a caricature of the painter Whistler, incorporating his eyeglass and hairstyle, Oscar Wilde's mannerisms and knee breeches and Walter Crane's velvet coat.

D'Oyly Carte issued a circular in 1881:

"I have pleasure to announce that my opera company is about to visit your neighbourhood. The 'movement' in the direction of a more artistic feeling, which had its commencement sometime since

Full length portrait of Oscar Wilde by Napoleon Saroni, around 1882. From the Library of Congress collection.

in the works of Mr Ruskin and his supporters, doubtless did much to render our everyday existence more pleasant and beautiful. Latterly, however, their pure and healthy teaching has given place to the outpourings of a clique of professors of ultra refinement, who preach the gospel or morbid languor and sickly sensuousness, which is half real and half affected by its high priests for the purpose of gaining social notoriety. Generally speaking, the new school is distinguished by an eccentricity of taste tending to an unhealthy admiration for exhaustion, corruption and decay. In satirising the excesses of these (so-called) aesthetes the authors of *Patience* have not desired to cast ridicule on the true aesthetic spirit, but only to attack the unmanly oddities which masquerade in its likeness. In doing so, they have succeeded in producing one of the prettiest and most diverting musical pleasantries of the day."

So there it was; an attack on the overly affected and trendy figureheads and fashions of the time. The opera would have a military sound. It would pit aestheticism against militarism and, to the horror of the Dragoons in the story, women would prefer the aesthetic.

Sullivan wrote the music to *Patience* in Nice and finished it off just before the opening when he had returned to England. The orchestration took 10 days and the score was sent to the theatre piece by piece. Sullivan knew that Gilbert often cut numbers, even up to final rehearsal and he had learned from experience that it was best to wait until the last minute to see which pieces would be in the opera, rather than waste his time on material that would not be used.

As it was, rather than alienating individuals like Oscar Wilde, he actually went to see the opera. D'Oyly Carte organised an American tour for him and he was a member of the audience when *Patience* was put on at the Standard Theatre in the New Year. Cannily, D'Oyly Carte also organised Wilde's lecture tour to coincide with performances of *Patience* in particular US cities.

Detail from a May 1881 issue of Punch, *showing Gilbert and Sullivan.*

Patience

The opera opened at the Opera Comique on April 23, a Saturday, and two days later, on April 25, 1881, *The Times* ran a review:

"Messrs. Gilbert and Sullivan's new extravaganza, produced at the Opera Comique on Saturday, deals with the fashion, or, as some will have it, the craze generally termed 'æsthetic'. To define the meaning of that word in this technical sense would not be quite easy. That the group of highly gifted artists and poets who have in many respects beautified the surroundings of English life do not come under the category of 'æsthetes' Mr. Gilbert would probably be the first to allow. What he and other satirists try to ridicule is not the movement itself, but rather the exaggerated and ridiculous form it takes among persons who, without natural taste of their own, try to assume the attitudes and mimic the appearance of their intellectual superiors. From this point of view the aim of the opera may be fully approved of.

Neither must it surprise us that Mr. Gilbert at this comparatively late hour should enter a field so successfully cultivated by others. His racy and individual sense of humour might be expected to discover new and quaint aspects even after all that has been read and seen in the columns of *Punch*. Mr. Du Maurier and Mr. Burnand have anticipated him in many respects. The antics and the jargon of imaginary 'æsthetic' circles have become familiar as household words. But still it remained that Postlethwaite, after having being admired in a pictorial and a dramatic capacity, should at last become vocal, and this feat the united efforts of Mr. Gilbert and Mr. Sullivan have achieved.

There is indeed in the new piece a dualism of the Postlethwaite principle represented by Mr. Reginald Bunthorne, a 'fleshly poet' (Mr. Gilbert should have avoided the meaningless and offensive epithet), and by Mr. Archibald Grosvenor, an 'idyllic poet', his compeer and his rival in the affections of a chorus of rapturous maidens of title. Patience, a dairymaid, gives the title to the play, and supplies the contrast of healthy ignorance of æsthetic idealities. Colonel Calverley (somewhat resembling the familiar type of 'our friend the colonel' in *Punch*), and other officers of the Dragoon

Guards, represent another phase of realistic opposition till they also assume the garb of mediæval bards to win the favour of the rapturous maidens.

The scene of the play, we should add, has been transferred from the drawing-room of the Cimabue Browns to a glade near Castle Bunthorne, situated, it would appear, in that undiscovered country of whimsical fancy in which Mr. Gilbert is so thoroughly at home. A story that can be told in plain prose would be out of place in such surroundings, and we shall not attempt to assign a local habitation and a name to what is obviously and purposely an airy nothing. It

Lady Angela and Lady Saphir in Patience, *from an 1881 New York Poster. From the Library of Congress collection.*

will be better to give the outline of some of the characters and types which Mr. Gilbert has drawn forth from his inner consciousness, for it would be difficult to identify them with anybody or anything that ever has existed or under any circumstances could exist.

There is, in the first place, Reginald Bunthorne, the æsthetic or fleshly poet, who expounds the mysteries of his heart to a bevy of twenty love-sick maidens, receiving in return their passionate devotion. Of Mr. Bunthorne's effusions several specimens are given, notably a song somewhat in the Rabelaisian vein, setting forth, among other things, that poetry and the tender passion are but forms of indigestion, curable by 'colocynth and calomel'. The lines are neither very refined nor very witty, and all the more disappointing if one considers how amusing a clever parody of certain tricks and mannerisms of modern poetry might have been made. The love-sick maidens, however, are of a different opinion. To them Bunthorne's work appears 'purely fragrant', 'earnestly precious', and they soundly rate their admirers, the Dragoon officers, for failing to be 'Empyrean, Della Cruscan, or even Early English'.

The poet, it need scarcely be added, treats the admiration of his fair votaries with scorn. His passion, he declares, is fixed on Patience, the milkmaid, who, on her part, does not appreciate the raptures of the poet, and, indeed, is totally insensible to the pangs of passion until a new hero appears on the scene in the shape of Archibald Grosvenor, another bard of the æsthetic school, who has made the simple and pastoral his speciality and recites 'decalets' about 'Gentle Jane was good as gold', and 'Teasing Tom was a very bad boy' to the enraptured maidens. For these fickle damozels have without a moment's hesitation transferred the allegiance from the lean and languid Bunthorne to the handsome Grosvenor.

One lady, however, has remained faithful to her first idol. This is the Lady Jane, a damsel of mature and highly developed charms, who soliloquises to this effect, accompanying herself on a gigantic violoncello the while:– 'The fickle crew have deserted Reginald, because he has glanced with favour on a puling milkmaid! Fools! Of that fancy he will soon weary, and then I, who alone am faithful to him, shall reap my reward. But do not dally too long, Reginald, for

I am ripe, Reginald, and already I am decaying. Better secure me ere I have gone too far.'

How the Lady Jane is ultimately rewarded by becoming the bride, not of Reginald, but of a 'duke with a thousand a day'; how the heavy Dragoons, after transforming themselves for a season into æsthetic worshippers finally regain their uniforms and their fickle lady loves; how Patience, after loving the unsympathetic Bunthorne from motives of duty finds happiness in the arms of the irresistible Archibald – all this is set forth in the course of the piece. The dénouement Mr. Gilbert has borrowed from his own incomparable ballad of the Rival Curates. For, like the Rev. Hopley Porter 'doing it on compulsion', Archibald doffs the uncomfortable garb of the æsthetic bard and appears at the end of the play in his natural shape as –

'An everyday young man;
A commonplace type
With a stick and a pipe
And a half-bred black and tan;
Who thinks suburban 'hops'
More fun than 'Monday Pops,'
Whose fond of his dinner,
And doesn't get thinner,
On bottled beer and chops.'

We are conscious that the bare outline of Mr. Gilbert's fanciful characters we have endeavoured to draw gives but a very imperfect idea of the quality of the plot, lit up as it is by the incessant fireworks of his wit and humour. In this kind of pyrotechnic display the new piece is certainly not inferior to anything that has preceded it from the same pen. There is, indeed, a perfect embarras de richesses of truly humorous sayings and doings, as harmless as they are laughter-compelling. We need scarcely add that there is not a sentence in the dialogue which, to use Mr. Archibald Grosvenor's words of his decalet, 'is calculated to bring the blush of shame to the cheek of modesty', the superiority in this as in other respects, of English over French burlesque being again manifested in the most striking manner.

As a piece of extravagant fun, Mr. Gilbert's new piece is simply admirable; as a satirical picture of a certain phase of modern life it cannot be recognized. There is scarcely a trace of poetic, artistic, or even social aspects of æstheticism. Mr. Gilbert has shown his taste in avoiding distinct personal references of any kind; but even the general features of the original, which, to judge by the denomination of his 'æsthetic opera' he intended to portray, seem to have escaped him. The poetry of Reginald Bunthorne is totally unlike anything published by any real poet in England; even the dresses and colours of the rapturous maidens (not excepting the

The character Reginald Bunthorne in Patience, *from a New York print of a colour woodcut dated 1881. From the Library of Congress collection.*

69

peacock embroidered gown of the formidable Lady Jane), would scarcely pass muster in an æsthetic drawing-room. Such at least will probably be the impression of most observers in this country; in America no doubt the new opera will be hailed with welcome as a faithful counterfeit presentment of London society.

With regard to Mr. Sullivan's music we can speak more briefly. Not that its merits are in any way inferior to those of the poetry. The two ingredients will in this, as in previous cases, combine to secure the success which may be safely prognosticated for the new opera. The difficulties of Mr. Sullivan's position in his collaboration with Mr. Gilbert have previously been insisted upon. Mr. Gilbert's dialogue is made up of wit and point and verbal quibble; and music knows nothing of wit and humour. All that can be done, and that Mr. Sullivan does with consummate skill, is to supply flowing and pretty tunes for melodious or rattling lines, as the case may be. That so skilful a writer for the orchestra, moreover, does not miss any opportunities for instrumental characterization it is almost unnecessary to add. Thus the dragoons are duly announced by the flourish of trumpets, and a kind of pastoral leitmotiv, assigned to the wood wind, accompanies the idyllic poet.

It is, moreover, curious to observe how, as soon as any chance offers, music resumes her natural attitude as the purest and most earnest of arts. We are referring less to such sentimental ditties as the pretty ballad of Patience, 'Love is a plaintive song,' than, for example, to the charming little duet between that young lady and the poet Grosvenor. Here the purport of the poetry is distinctly humorous, and the refrain, 'Hey, but I'm doleful, willow, willow, waly,' may be cited as one of those weak attempts at parody, which apply as it happens to Shakespeare at least as much as to Mr. Swinburne. But Mr. Sullivan's music very properly ignores all this; it takes everything seriously, and the result is an exquisite ditty in that 'Early English' style, which Mr. Gilbert tries to ridicule. Even the finale of the first act – clever caricature of the conventional operatic finale as it is – might well be accepted as a genuine tragic action by a naïve audience un-provided with the book of words. The same finale, by the way, Mr. Sullivan might easily have turned to better musical account than he has done. The piece is lengthily rather than organically developed, and the unaccompanied sestet is no more than a pretty tune sung in harmony.

The overture also leaves something to be desired. It is made up of themes from the opera loosely strung together, the principal motive showing a striking resemblance to a familiar melody from Nicolai's *Merry Wives of Windsor*. But in spite of all this, Mr. Sullivan's workmanship is infinitely above the level of opéra bouffe as imported from abroad. One may regret that a musician of his power should occupy so much of his time with this class of composition; at the same time it is a matter for congratulation that in England the demand for burlesque opera is supplied in a refined and truly artistic manner.

Reasons of space compel us to speak of the performance with great brevity. The opera was produced under the personal direction of author and composer, and its rendering may, therefore, be accepted as representative. Most of the artists in the cast are, moreover, well known to the frequenters of the Opera Comique. Mr. George Grossmith, dressed in the early Florentine garb, familiarized by Sir Frederick Leighton's illustrations to Romola, looked and acted the æsthetic poet, Reginald Bunthorne, to perfection, Mr. Rutland Barrington being his worthy brother bard in the 'idyllic' line. Colonel Calverley of the 35th Dragoons (Mr. Richard Temple) was as dashing a soldier and as sentimental an 'æsthete' as the most rapturous maiden could expect in her varying moods; Mr. Frank Thornton, his major, and Mr. Durward Lely, his lieutenant, endeavouring to follow in the footsteps of their superior officer. Miss Leonora Braham (Patience) was a sweet-voiced milkmaid, whose appearance suggested that she had stepped from one of Mr. Walter Crane's or Mr. Caldecott's picture-books; but, perhaps, the most remarkable piece of acting was Miss Alice Barnett's Lady Jane, a masterpiece of humorous impersonation. Of the success of the piece on the first night – of the incessant applause, the encores, the calls before the curtain – it would be difficult to give an idea."

In all, *Patience* would run for 578 performances and it was described as a new and original aesthetic opera in two acts, with the subtitle *Bunthorne's Bride*.

The Colonel in Patience, *from a New York 1881 poster.* From the Library of Congress collection.

Patience Cast and Synopsis

Colonel Calverley	Richard Temple
Major Murgatroyd	Frank Thornton
Lieutenant the Duke of Dunstable	Durward Lely
Reginald Bunthorne	George Grossmith
Archibald Grosvenor	Rutland Barrington
Bunthorne's Solicitor	George Bowley
Lady Angela	Jessie Bond
Lady Saphir	Julia Gwynne
Lady Ella	May Fortescue
Lady Jane	Alice Barnett
Patience	Leonora Braham

Act I

Lovesick maidens are gathered outside Bunthorne Castle but Bunthorne is already in love with the village milkmaid, Patience. Patience has no idea why the maidens are so unhappy and she tells them that the Dragoon Guards have just returned to the village; the maidens were engaged to them last year. Patience cannot understand why the maidens are not excited and the Dragoons cannot believe that the maidens are obsessed with the poet. This is reinforced when they actually see him. Bunthorne is pretending to be an aesthetic in order to attract attention and he cannot understand why Patience does not return his feelings of love. Patience asks Lady Angela to explain to her what true love really means. She tells her that love is unselfish and Patience realises that to

Lady Jane in Patience, *from a 1881 poster print from New York.* From the Library of Congress collection.

deny her love would be selfish. She comes across Archibald Grosvenor, who tries to woe her and she discovers that he is one of her old childhood friends. Grosvenor is loved by many women and Patience comes to the conclusion that to love him would be selfish. A heartbroken Bunthorne decides to raffle himself, but before the prize raffle can be drawn Patience tells him that to love him would not be selfish and that she will accept him. Bunthorne is delighted and the other maidens return to their former lovers, the Dragoon, but only until they see Grosvenor.

Act II

Lady Jane, an elderly spinster, still loves Bunthorne and hopes that he will tire of Patience and return her love. Grosvenor is extremely unhappy. The maidens beg him to read poetry to them. Bunthorne is angry about the maidens' betrayal and is concerned about Patience's interest in Grosvenor, so he decides to confront the man. At a loss about what to do the Dragoons dress up as aesthetics and the maidens are interested and promise that they will return to the Dragoons if Grosvenor does not choose one of them as a lover. Meanwhile Bunthorne and Grosvenor argue. Finally Grosvenor agrees to stop dressing and behaving as an aesthetic; Bunthorne is delighted. In return, Bunthorne decides that he will become more cheerful and approachable, thus making himself perfect. This means that Patience, because of his perfection, cannot love him as this would be selfish. Therefore she turns to Grosvenor. The Dragoons win back their maidens and although Lady Jane still loves Bunthorne she is wooed by the Duke of Dunstable. Lady Jane is attracted by the prospect of becoming a duchess and abandons Bunthorne, who is the only character at the end of the play not to have a partner.

Savoy Theatre

Richard D'Oyly Carte issued a prospectus for his new theatre. He had recognised that the Opera Comique was not only too small but was also too old-fashioned. Above all he hated turning people away at the door:

'The Savoy Theatre is placed between the Strand and the Victoria Embankment, on a plot of land of which I have purchased the freehold, and is built on a spot possessing many associations of historic interest, being close to the Savoy Chapel and in the 'precinct of the Savoy', where stood formerly the Savoy Palace, once inhabited by John of Gaunt and the Dukes of Lancaster, and made memorable in the Wars of the Roses. On the Savoy manor there was formerly a theatre. I have used the ancient name as an appropriate title for the present one. The theatre is large and commodious, but little smaller than the Gaiety, and will seat 1,292 persons. I think I may claim to have carried out some improvements deserving special notice. The most important of these are in the lighting and decoration. From the time, now some years since, that the first electric lights in lamps were exhibited outside the Paris Opera House, I have been convinced that electric light in some form is the light of the future for use in theatres, not to go further. There are several extremely good incandescent lamps, but I finally decided to adopt that of Mr J W Swan, the well known inventor of Newcastle on Tyne. The enterprise of Messrs Siemens Bros Co has enabled me to try the experiment of exhibiting this light in my theatre. About 1,200 lights are used, and the power to generate a sufficient current for these is obtained from large steam engines, giving about 120 in full horse power, placed on some open land near the theatre. The new light is not only used in the audience part of the theatre, but on stage, for footlights, side and top lights, etc. And (not of the least importance for the comfort of the performers) in the dressing rooms – in fact in every part of the house. This is the first time that it has been attempted to light any public building entirely by electricity.'

This was the first time any theatre had had internal electrics. There were still some concerns about electricity and to comfort them D'Oyly Carte guaranteed that gaslights would be laid on as an alternative. It also got over another major problem with theatres; foul air and heat. Gas burners consumed oxygen and were hot. The new lamps did neither of these things.

The new theatre would open on October 10, 1881, with an even bigger and better version of *Patience*. The scenery needed to be repainted and Gilbert set about reorganising the production, as there was a far bigger stage. Not only was the new production a triumph, but it also meant that other individuals in different industries and walks of life were animated by the prospect of an electrified theatre. This meant that the opera was even reviewed and commented upon by journals as unconnected to theatre as *The Electrical Times*.

The creation of the theatre did cause problems between the three partners. D'Oyly Carte had built the theatre using his own funds. The existing three-man partnership would split the profits of the operas, but that was after a rent of £4,000 per year had been taken out.

The theatre had been designed by the architect C J Phipps and it went up in a matter of months, in red brick and Portland stone. It had a circle without pillars, it was spacious and nearly every seat had a perfect view of the stage.

It was the policy of the theatre to pay the attendants decent wages; tips were abolished and programmes handed out at no cost. Queues were

The Savoy Theatre, which faces the embankment in London.

organised for un-booked seats, the seating was in deep blue, the backs of the boxes in Venetian red, the stage curtains in yellow satin. There were entrances to the theatre on all four sides, there was a black and white, marble, circular entrance area, a refreshment saloon, a lounge for the ladies and a smoking room. The stage for the Savoy was illuminated with electricity for the very first time for the matinee performance on December 28, 1881.

Patience would prove to be extremely popular; arguably it had better songs than the previous Gilbert and Sullivan efforts. The partnership sent out companies to tour around Britain, America and Australia. From the proceeds Sullivan moved into Queen's Mansions in Victoria Street and Gilbert had a large house built in Harrington Gardens in South Kensington. Gilbert had central heating, a bathroom on each floor and a telephone.

Iolanthe

By 1882 Gilbert and Sullivan were immensely rich, earning twice as much as the Prime Minister, Gladstone. Sullivan in particular liked to freely spend his money on travel, horse racing and in the casino. Gilbert wrote to Sullivan on February 16, 1882:

'My telephone is fixed and in working order – it costs £20 per annum. They are fixing one at the theatre, and it will be finished this week. Shall I order one for you? It takes some time, four or five weeks, to finish. I have ordered an instrument to be fixed at the prompt entrance so that I shall be able to hear the performance from my study – so will you, from your house, if you decide to have one. I am hard at work on Act II but have infinite difficulty with it.'

In fact by the time this letter reached Sullivan he was in Egypt; he had left with Arthur Clay onboard HMS *Hercules*. They were guests of the Duke of Edinburgh on a voyage to the Baltic. They visited Copenhagen, Russia and then sailed into Kiel in Germany. Sullivan then returned to London and went off to Egypt for three months, as he was fascinated by Arab music.

Meanwhile Gilbert was working hard on the libretto for *Iolanthe*. It would become a combination of political satire and fairy magic, incorporating mortals and immortals. The initial idea for the opera was based on Gilbert's own *The Fairy Curate*, which featured the marriage between a fairy and a solicitor. He originally intended the Fairy Queen to marry the Prime Minister and have the whole opera set in the House of Commons. He then switched it so that it would be based in the House of Lords.

Sullivan's mother fell ill in May 1882 and died. He wrote in his diary on June 1 that he was feeling very lonely, but just two days later he began work on *Iolanthe*. Sullivan managed to complete the overture in the early morning of November 24, 1882. That very evening was a dress rehearsal that would run from 7 in the evening until 1:30 the next morning; the very day of the first performance. There was dreadful news for Sullivan on November 25, 1882, as his diary disclosed:

'Received letter from E A Hall saying that he was ruined and my money (about £7,000) lost, just before starting for the theatre. Dined with Smythe at home. First performance of *Iolanthe* at the Savoy Theatre. House crammed – awfully nervous, more so than usual on going into the orchestra. Tremendous reception. First act went splendidly – the second dragged and I was afraid it must be compressed. However it finished well and Gilbert and myself were called and heartily cheered. Very low afterwards – came home.'

The *Morning Advertiser* reviewed *Iolanthe* on Monday, November 27, 1882:

'"Patience" having had an unusually long run, the bill at the Savoy is changed. A new fairy opera, "Iolanthe; or, the Peer and the Peri," by Messrs. Gilbert and Sullivan, was brought out on Saturday night. It was a success, but the second of the two acts will bear cutting.

The opera is written on the lines laid down by Mr. W. S. Gilbert, and no greater compliment can be paid him than to say that his libretto will bear reading. In point of fact, the enjoyment of those who go to see "Iolanthe" will be considerably enhanced by perusal of the text, which is full of those quaint conceits and piquant fancies peculiar to the author. This "Iolanthe" shows no strong or radical departure from the previous style and method of procedure adopted with such profitable results by Mr. Gilbert in the dramatic framework supplied to Mr. Sullivan. Neither of them strikes out anything particularly novel in design. The paths they have trodden are still open to them, and they wisely elect not to diverge from the track too soon.

The Gilbertian school of humour is unique and peculiar. It may not endure, but it has made its mark. Neither Mr. Gilbert as an author, nor Mr. Sullivan as a musician, write for immortality. The school they have founded may not, perhaps, last far beyond their own time; nor can it be said that their operas are likely to confer any benefit upon the future lyric stage. They write for the time, and leave more elevated forms of art to the care of others. For all that, their work is most valuable, and has a distinctly beneficial influence. If they do no more than the majority of their fellows for the eternal glory of the musical drama, they do not degrade it.

Their operas have nothing in common with the inanities of modern burlesque. Burlesques they certainly are in a way, but free from vulgarity, commonplace, or coarseness, direct or inferential. Mr. Gilbert does not forget that he is writing for English women. He is not unwarrantably suggestive, even in his wildest and most eccentric flights of fancy; that is a great point.

Coming to the technicalities of writing, his versification is perfect. His rhymes are invariably true, his dialogue carefully polished, and no slipshod sentences are to be found from one to the other end of any play of his. As usual, in "Iolanthe" he turns human nature upside down, indulges in the most violent outrages against common sense, and puts before us a diverting jumble of the real and the ideal — of prosaic, every-day life, treated from the facetious point of view, and the fantastic proceedings of the fairies. He revels in producing violent contrasts, ultra-ridiculous surprises, and in misrepresenting everything as it exists in human nature. No idea is too ludicrous for Mr. Gilbert to originate and work out, no situation too absurd in which to place his characters. This opera, like some of its predecessors, is a kind of exaggerated Bab ballad. The behaviour of every soul in it is intensely unreasonable. Probability, or even possibility, is held of no moment, and is systematically despised. Folly shakes her bells, and reason is beaten out of the field; but in his wildest moments, Mr. Gilbert is the keen satirist. He has a way of bringing truths before his audience, while seeming to desire nothing better than to make them laugh. He turns human nature the seamy side without, but mirthfully; he is not simply a laborious punster, and twister of words, but in his way is an analyzer of character, and a true if severe commentator on the weaknesses, the meanness, and the shame of the world and of men.

Bearing witness to Mr. Gilbert's power as a perfectly original humorist, it must be confessed that he sometimes repeats himself, and daringly, too, not so much in the letter as in the spirit. No author with the least pride in his work would, of course, venture upon direct reproduction of himself, but a form of joke that has once told well is not always readily abandoned. In this opera, the Lord Chancellor, one of the characters, has a speech of self-examination, somewhat of that given to the lady in "Engaged," who cannot quite satisfy herself as to whose wife she is. Again a capital song, given to the Chancellor, is to some extent suggestive of that in which the Judge in "Trial by Jury," details his upward progress in the legal profession.

As for telling the plot of "Iolanthe," we may claim exemption from that task. The whole thing is one of those extended jokes to be heartily enjoyed, but not to be described in the ordinary way. The main idea is that the Lord Chancellor of England is in love with one of his wards. Mr. Gilbert elaborates this quite in his own manner, and constantly brings mortals and immortals together in most diverting fashion.

Miss Leonora Braham plays Phyllis, a typical shepherdess of Arcadia, and of the Dresden china pattern. Her lover is called Strephon, the offspring of a fairy condemned to live at the bottom of a river for marrying a mortal, but released at the intercession of a bevy of long-skirted Fays, reigned over by a massive Queen (Miss Alice Barnett). As in the "Pirates of Penzance" and "Patience," the lady's stature and proportions are made the subject of many jokes that tell fully with the audience. Miss Barnett is made up in a golden helmet, and looks something like Brunnhilde in the Wagnerian opera. The stately Queen ends by proposing to and marrying a Grenadier Guard, sentry in Palace-yard, Westminster.

This is a tolerably wild notion among many others Mr. Gilbert puts into form.

The scene of the first act is a remarkably pretty rustic landscape with practicable bridge. After Strephon and Phyllis, the flageolet-playing rustics, have appeared, the stage becomes filled with a numerous company of English peers, all in their robes, and everyone of them in love with the shepherdess. The entrance of these noblemen, cloaked and gartered and coroneted, is the most absurd thing conceivable. They are preceded by the band of the Grenadiers, and accompanied by the Lord Chancellor (Mr. Grossmith), who finds himself in the extraordinary position of being of being obliged to ask his own consent to marry his fascinating ward Phyllis. He has an exceedingly humorous song, "The law is the true embodiment;" another even better, "When I went to the Bar as a very young man;" and a third, "When you're lying awake," in the second act. On Saturday night all were encored, and this will probably be the case at future representations, for Mr. Grossmith sings them with great point and remarkable clearness of articulation. In this second act the solemn representative of English law, the all-powerful Chancellor, tucks up his robes and joins in a wild dance with two of the peers — Earl Tolloller (Mr. Durward Lely) and the Earl of Mountararat (Mr. Rutland Barrington). A trio, of which this ridiculous dance forms part, was re-demanded, evidently on account of the intense absurdity of the situation, although it came late in the evening.

The ludicrous is drawn upon freely by Mr. Gilbert from first to last. Thus we have the robust Strephon with a fairy mother, Iolanthe (Miss Jessie Bond), looking considerably younger than himself.

At the very commencement of the second act, a stalwart Grenadier (Mr. Manners), on guard opposite Westminster Hall, has a song, "When all night long a chap remains." This, both words and music, is conceived in the best and truest spirit of burlesque. Both the dramatist and the musician are also to be congratulated on the last song of the Chancellor, "When you're lying awake." Nowadays comic songs frequently find their way into drawing-rooms, and this is one that will no doubt be extensively taken up. It might be sung in any assemblage.

The opera contains surprises in plenty, and one that came with singular effect on Saturday night. Those who had books of the words came in due course to a kind of Bab ballad, and in Mr. Gilbert's best vein "De Belleville was regarded as the Crichton of his age." It fell to the lot of Lord Mountararat, and everyone of course thought Mr. Barrington would sing it. To the intense surprise, however, of the audience, the facetious ballad was recited. It should have made a stronger mark than it did, for it is very cleverly written. The middle verse was omitted, which was a pity, for not a line of so good a thing should be lost.

In this act is a dainty little duet for two of the principal fairies, Celia and Leila (Miss Fortescue and Miss Julia Gwynne), supported by the chorus. It has a charmingly fanciful and piquant accompaniment for the strings pizzicato, and is more than a credit to Mr. Arthur Sullivan. Strange to say, this pretty duet was allowed to go almost unnoticed. A song for the Fairy Queen almost immediately succeeding the duet, has, as a choral refrain, a sham lachrymose appeal to Captain Shaw, head of the London Fire Brigade. This may not seem in the telling to suggest much of the facetious, but the effect of the fairies calling dolorously upon the gallant captain is indescribably funny. It is in consequence intensely absurd, and one of those literary vagaries that only Mr. Gilbert could venture upon. All the characters have solos, in which Mr. Arthur Sullivan's gift of melody puts itself agreeably in evidence.

Strephon and Phyllis each begin with a pretty little pastoral, one a repetition of the other. Here and in every other number of the opera, concerted music or otherwise, the supporting orchestration is refined and elegant. Some of Mr. Sullivan's previous operas have contained music more calculated to take at once the public ear, but the score of "Iolanthe" is worthy of the composer, and the finale to the first act is full of brightness, and very cleverly written. The overture, too, is very good. At first the audience did not seem to be very strongly interested, but the entry of the Peers, made up with the modern whiskers above their splendid mantles and dresses, soon put matters upon a different footing. From this facetious point onwards to nearly the close of the opera everything went merrily.

Left: *The original programme from the first run of* Iolanthe, *1882.*

Below: *The inside of the programme for the original run of Gilbert and Sullivan's* Iolanthe, *1882.*

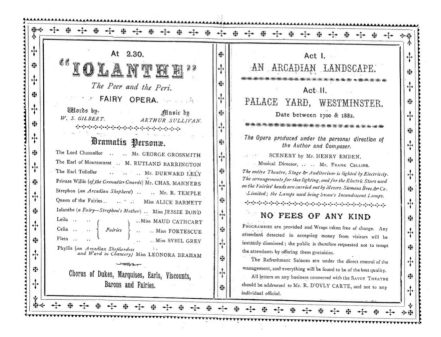

The last scene dragged a little, but it will not be difficult to cut it slightly, and bring the action more closely together. In the last scene a very brilliant and original effect is introduced. The Fairy Queen and her three chief attendants wear each an electric star in their hair. The effect of this brilliant spark of electricity is wonderful. Coruscations of the electric light were introduced, if we remember rightly, in a dark fir forest scene at the Princess's, some few years ago, but this is a new development, and a perfect success. "Iolanthe" is well done throughout. Miss Leonora Braham seemed a little out of voice, but is quite equal to the part of Phyllis, which she plays naturally and agreeably. Miss Barnett makes a capital Fairy Queen, and shows a true appreciation of humour. Misses Fortescue, Gwynne, and Sybil Grey are pretty and graceful fairies. Mr. George Grossmith's Lord Chancellor is rich in quiet, unforced drollery, and the rest of the gentlemen artists do well in their several characters. The moonlight scene of Palace-yard, Westminster, is an excellent example of stage illusion. Mr. Sullivan conducted, and received an ovation on taking his seat in the orchestra. With Mr. Gilbert he was called on at the end of the performance. The like compliment was paid to Mr. D'Oyly Carte, who has spared no expense in mounting the opera.'

Iolanthe Cast and Synopsis

Although the first Gilbert and Sullivan opera to be performed at the Savoy Theatre was *Patience*, *Iolanthe* was the first one to be written for the Savoy's stage. The first performance got underway on November 25, 1882 and the audience was amazed to see battery operated lamps fixed to the fairy's heads for additional magic effect. The peers that appeared had hidden wings underneath their robes, which were revealed by pulling hidden cords.

The Lord Chancellor	George Grossmith
Earl of Mountararat	Rutland Barrington
Earl Tolloller	Derward Lely
Private Willis	Charles Manners
Strephon	Richard Temple
Queen of the Fairies	Alice Barnett

Iolanthe	Jessie Bond
Celia	May Fortescue
Leila	Julia Gwynne
Fleta	Sybil Grey
Phyllis	Leonora Braham

Act I

An Arcadian landscape. Iolanthe, a fairy, has been banished and the inhabitants of fairyland are sad. She had married a mortal 25 years before and instead of being sentenced to death for this crime she had been banished for penal servitude for life. The Fairy Queen is finally persuaded to pardon Iolanthe, but Iolanthe is somewhat unwilling because she wants to be near to her son, Strephon, who is a shepherd. He wants to marry Phyllis. Phyllis agrees to meet him and they discuss their wedding plans. Members of the House of Lords arrive, followed by the Lord Chancellor. The Lords love Phyllis and she is summoned to them; despite their proposals she tells them that she is already in love with Strephon. The Lord Chancellor is angry and he refuses to give his consent to the marriage. Iolanthe, who looks younger than even her own son, comforts Strephon and everyone jumps to the wrong conclusion and believes that he is being unfaithful to Phyllis. Phyllis offers her love to Tolloller and Mountararat. In desperation Strephon calls the fairies to help. They scold the Lords and try to set things straight. The Lords do not believe them and the Fairy Queen reveals who she really is and threatens to ensure that Strephon becomes a member of parliament and says she will give him powers to pass any law.

Act II

Palace yard, Westminster. The scene opens with Private Willis, a soldier in the Grenadier Guards, thinking about his life. The Lords are angered by Strephon's abilities and neither Tolloller nor Mountararat can decide who should marry Phyllis. To add to the confusion the Lord Chancellor has also fallen in love with her, but as she is his ward he cannot make his feelings known. Strephon is depressed, despite his abilities. He meets with Phyllis and tells her that his mother is a fairy. Phyllis now realises what a dreadful mistake she has made. Iolanthe now confesses that the Lord Chancellor is her husband, but that she cannot disclose herself to him as this is against fairy law. The Lord Chancellor fails to stop Strephon and Phyllis from running away, and Iolanthe disguises herself again. Despite Iolanthe's pleas the Lord Chancellor wants to marry Phyllis, so Iolanthe tells him that she is his wife, the punishment for which is death. The Fairy Queen arrives but before she can pronounce the sentence she discovers that the other fairies have married members of the Lords, so she must kill them all. The Lord Chancellor offers to change the law so that it means that a fairy must marry a mortal or be killed. The Fairy Queen agrees with him and is attracted to Private Willis. He sprouts wings and everyone flies off to live in fairyland.

All was not particularly well financially, and as we have seen Sullivan had lost an enormous amount of money. But Gilbert too was outraged by spiralling costs. He wrote to Sullivan:

> 'Our quarterly division has just been made, and I find that our nightly expenses are £130 per night! This is outrageous and I have written a letter to Carte, of which I enclose a copy, and which will convey to you my ideas on the subject of retrenchment. A short code is appended, and I wish you would wire me according to the code that I may be sure I am acting in accordance with your wishes. If you and Carte agree on any one point I shall of course consider it decided, and act accordingly.'

In his letter to D'Oyly Carte Gilbert wrote:

> 'It is all very well while we are playing to £250 nightly, but when business drops the consequences may be very serious. The gas bill at the Savoy costs £10 a week more than at the Comique – and this with electric light! If we play for a year to an average of 120 nightly receipts, we make at the Opera Comique £9,000 a year – and we lose at the Savoy £3,000 a year. You will see at once that this is simple ruination.'

Iolanthe would run for 398 performances. Literally thousands of copies of the vocal and piano scores were sold.

Gladstone was amongst those who thoroughly enjoyed the performance of *Iolanthe* and in the spring of 1883 he would write to Sullivan, offering him a knighthood. The ceremony would take place at Windsor Castle on May 22, 1883. In the same month Sullivan celebrated his forty first birthday and amongst the guests were Gilbert, the Duke of Edinburgh and the Prince of Wales.

Princess Ida

Back in 1870 Gilbert had written a play based on Lord Tennyson's poem *The Princess*. He now used a lot of the dialogue, including the blank verse, to create the libretto for *Princess Ida*. Gilbert read part of Act I to Sullivan in February 1883 and at first he did not like it. But in time he warmed to the idea and on his first day composing the music he wrote two choruses and two songs. He was busy at the Leeds Festival that autumn and this held back work on *Princess Ida*. The target of Gilbert's satire in *Princess Ida* was women's emancipation and it was scheduled for production at the end of 1883.

Also there was a significant event on February 8, 1883, which involved the signing of an agreement between Gilbert and Sullivan and D'Oyly Carte; it was an agreement that would last for five years and could be extended. It was to become the contract that was in dispute in the famous Carpet Quarrel, which blew up in 1890. Leslie Baily, the author of *The Gilbert and Sullivan Book* (Cassell 1952) explained the significance of the contract:

'It gave Carte a licence for the performance at the Savoy Theatre of operas composed by Gilbert and Sullivan, Carte agreeing to pay to each of them one third of the net profit earned, after deducting £4,000 a year rent for the theatre, and necessary expenses, including repairs incidental to the performance. The accounts were to be made up every three months, and the net profits paid to Gilbert and Sullivan were to be retained for their own use and not returned on account of any after loss, except any loss which might be incurred by a new opera not being produced in due time. Gilbert and Sullivan agreed not to write for any other theatre, and D'Oyly Carte not to produce the operas of any other authors.'

Straight after the Leeds Festival Sullivan headed back to London. He also had to cope with the sudden death of his friend Frederick Clay.

Nonetheless he was at the Savoy Theatre on New Year's Day, four days before the first performance of *Princess Ida*. He still had to write two songs. In his diary he wrote an entry dated January 5, 1884:

'Resolved to conduct the first performance of the new opera *Princess Ida* at night, but from the state I was in it seemed hopeless. At 7pm had another strong hypodermic injection to ease the pain, and a strong cup of black coffee to keep me awake. Managed to get up and dressed, and drove to the theatre more dead than alive – went into the orchestra at 8.10. Tremendous house – usual reception. Very fine performance – not a hitch. Brilliant success. After the performance I turned very faint and I could not stand.'

Sullivan was suffering from a great deal of muscle pain in the neck, but it was all linked to his old kidney problems. This event could have led to the end of Gilbert and Sullivan's partnership, as we will soon discover. *The Athenueum* reviewed *Princess Ida* on January 12, 1884:

'The last in the series of Messrs. Gilbert and Sullivan's fantastic operas contains so much that is clever and original that it is a pity its effect should be marred to some extent by clumsy arrangement. In its original form, Mr. Gilbert's "respectful perversion" of Tennyson's 'Princess' consisted of five scenes played without break in the ordinary burlesque style. It is now arranged in a prologue and two acts, the first and third divisions being brief, while the second is so abnormally long that a sense of fatigue cannot be resisted despite the author's whimsicalities and the composer's admirably conceived numbers. One or two of the lyrics could be spared, and with a little compression of the dialogue the piece will be improved in symmetry and balance. In the endeavour to assign to the new work its proper musical position in the list which begins with 'The Sorcerer,' we are reminded of the difficulty a composer must experience in maintaining any semblance of freshness in his method after working in one groove for so long a time. Sir Arthur Sullivan is not to be blamed because in 'Princess Ida' we meet with rhythms, phraseology, and tricks of orchestration which sound familiar. There is rather cause for wonder that in his latest effort there is so much that strikes the hearer as spontaneous, daintily expressed, and even beautiful. The composer is never more happy than when he reproduces the mannerisms of former musical epochs, and there are two or three numbers which will compare favourably with anything he has previously accomplished in this direction. The gem of the opera is the duet for Lady Blanche and Melissa, with its old-world grace; but scarcely inferior are a Handelian trio for the three sons of Gama, and a sham Anacreontic song for Cyril. In the concerted music Sir Arthur Sullivan displays a serious artistic purpose, and there is nothing that is unworthy of his reputation as a leading English musician. In this respect the new score will compare very favourably with that of 'H.M.S. Pinafore' – his first great success in collaboration with Mr. Gilbert. The performance is more noteworthy for general smoothness and good ensemble than for the special excellence of any individual member of the cast. Vocally, Miss L. Braham, Miss Chard, Mr. H. Bracy, and Mr. Durward Lely are most entitled to approving mention. Mr. Grossmith has less to do than usual, but he makes the most of his opportunities. The mounting of the piece is on the sumptuous scale always observed at Mr. D'Oyly Carte's theatre.'

Princess Ida opened on January 5, 1884 and its original run stretched for 246 performances. Its subtitle was *Castle Adamant*; this was a three act show.

Princess Ida Cast and Synopsis

King Hildebrand	Rutland Barrington
Hilarion	Henry Bracy
Cyril	Derward Lely
Florian	Charles Ryley
King Gama	George Grossmith
Arac	Richard Temple
Guron	Warwick Gray
Scynthius	William Lugg
Princess Ida	Leonora Braham
Lady Blanche	Rosina Brandram

Lady Psyche	Kate Chard
Melissa	Jessie Bond
Sacharissa	Sybil Grey
Chloe	Miss Heathcote
Ada	Miss Twyman

Act I

King Hildebrand is waiting for the neighbouring monarch, King Gama, to arrive. Gama's daughter, Ida, was betrothed as a child to Hilarion, Hildebrand's son. Just how Gama is greeted is dependent upon whether he brings Ida with him. He actually arrives with his three sons, Arac, Guron and Scynthius. Ida has not come because she has locked herself away in a castle, where she runs a university for women who teach that men are inferior. Hilarion decides to try to get into the university and win her love. He takes with him Cyril and Florian. In the meantime, Gama and his sons are held as hostage by Hildebrand.

Act II

The students at the university, known as Castle Adamant, are listening to a lecture about man being nature's mistake. It is being delivered by Lady Psyche, the professor of humanities. They then listen to Lady Blanche, the professor of abstract science. It is her role to punish women who bring men to the university or carry out usual women's tasks. Ida now arrives and explains why women are superior to men. Hilarion and his two friends climb over the castle wall and dress as undergraduates and make for Ida. Lady Psyche is Florian's sister and she recognises him. Melissa, who is Lady Blanche's daughter, is very curious as she has never seen men before. The two women decide to keep the secret but Lady Blanche herself is suspicious when she hears male voices. Melissa tells Lady Blanche that if she were to allow Hilarion to woe Ida then she would leave the university and Lady Blanche could take over. At lunchtime Cyril drinks too much and Ida, horrified, falls into the river; Hilarion rescues her. She has the three men arrested and then discovers that the castle is being besieged by Hildebrand and that her father and brothers are his hostages.

Act III

Ida refuses to surrender, but the students are not so confident and soon she is left alone. King Gama offers a solution; his three sons will fight Hilarion, Cyril and Florian. Gama's sons are beaten in the hand-to-hand combat. Ida now sees that the only sensible way forward is to go ahead with the marriage and to spend her life with Hilarion, thus pacifying the two warring kings.

Shortly after *Princess Ida* opened D'Oyly Carte received a letter from Sullivan, telling him that he would not write any more comic operas. Even after meeting with Sullivan, D'Oyly Carte still found him to be adamant; Sullivan was suffering from his kidney problems and decided to go abroad to convalesce.

During the time that the opera ran at the Savoy Gilbert had told the booking clerk to ring him each evening to let him know how much money had been taken. Gilbert too was worried about his abilities to turn in a significantly fresh sounding piece of work and was also concerned about the relatively poor box office takings. However he had already sketched out the libretto for a new opera when he heard that Sullivan was not interested in writing any more comic operas. Gilbert wrote to Sullivan, telling him that according to the contract they would be liable to pay D'Oyly Carte for any losses if they did not produce a new opera. By the time Gilbert's letter arrived Sullivan was in Paris and he wrote back:

'I will be quite frank. With *Princess Ida* I have come to the end of my tether – the end of my capability in that class of piece. My tunes are in danger of becoming mere repetitions of my former pieces, my concerted movements are getting to possess a strong family likeness. I have looked upon the words as being of such importance that I have been continually keeping down the music in order that not one should be lost. And this, my suppression is most difficult, most fatiguing, and I may say most disheartening, for the music is never allowed to rise and speak for itself. I want a chance for the music to act in its own proper sphere – to intensify the emotional element not only of the actual words but of the situation. I should like to set a story of human interest and probability, where the humorous words would come in a humorous (not serious) situation and where, if the situation were a tender or dramatic one the words would be of a similar character. There would then be a feeling of reality about it which would give fresh interest in writing, and fresh vitality to our joint work. I hope with all my heart that there may be no break in our chain of joint workmanship.'

Gilbert was quite taken aback and hurt by Sullivan's letter. With the audiences for *Princess Ida* falling off there would be a pressing need for Gilbert and Sullivan to produce something new to replace it. Sullivan appears to have come to the end of his tether and was frustrated that he was tied to Gilbert. Gilbert suggested that Sullivan could work with someone else on one piece of work, which might refresh their own partnership. Meetings between D'Oyly Carte and Gilbert and Sullivan failed to break the deadlock.

Suddenly Gilbert came up with the solution; he picked up a Japanese sword that was on the wall of his home in Harrington Gardens. He also knew that there was a Japanese exhibition on in London and he began to scribble down some basic ideas of a diminutive Japanese executioner carrying a big Japanese sword. He quickly dashed off a letter to Sullivan, suggesting a Japanese opera. Not only would the scenery and costumes be entirely different, but Sullivan would be able to write some unusual music.

On May 8, 1884 the reply from Sullivan arrived:

'Your letter is an inexpressible relief to me, as it clearly shows me that you, equally with myself, are loth to discontinue the collaboration which has been such a pleasure and advantage to us. If I understand you to propose you will construct a plot without the supernatural and improbable elements, and on the lines which you describe, I gladly undertake to set it without further discussing the matter, or asking what the subject is to be.'

Gilbert and Sullivan were about to embark on what would become arguably the most important of all of their operas. It was one of the most farfetched even though there were no supernatural or improbable elements. Everyone was relieved; it would be called *The Mikado*. It would not be ready in time to replace *Princess Ida*, so revivals of *The Sorcerer* and *Trial by Jury* were launched at the Savoy. The former, which had been only moderately successful in 1877, became a hit.

Before *Princess Ida* closed, however, an individual billed as H A Henri, just 17 years old, made his appearance in Glasgow. He was to become Henry A Lytton, who would have a long and successful career with The D'Oyly Carte Opera Company.

Chapter 5

Quarrels

Late Nineteenth Century Japan was still a strange, somewhat romantic and exciting country. For centuries it had remained apart from the rest of the world and only now were insights into Japan, its traditions and culture becoming known across the globe. It was extremely astute of Gilbert to create a new opera that coincided with this trend and the fact that there was a major Japanese exhibition in Knightsbridge in London.

The *Daily Telegraph* wrote, after the first night of *The Mikado*:

> 'The quaint arts of Nippon are faithfully reflected in the Gilbertian looking glass of *The Mikado* – in costume and scene, in the carefully-drilled flick of fans, the shuffling walk of the 'train of little ladies' – but when Mr Gilbert has taken you, like Alice, through his looking-glass and you gaze around expecting to find yourself in a foreign cherry-blossom land, you recognise things which are grotesquely familiar.'

Before the launch of *The Mikado*, on March 14 1885, the Savoy Theatre put on a double bill of *The Sorcerer* and *Trial by Jury*. This was quite an unusual event, as once operas had come to the end of their run it was rare to see them again. *The Mikado* by comparison would be the first opera to be recorded on disk in 1917. It also was to become the first Gilbert and Sullivan opera to be filmed, in 1938.

Gilbert left absolutely nothing to chance; he hired women from the Japanese exhibition to teach the performers how to bow, use a fan and walk. The Samurai sword from Gilbert's house became the principal prop used by George Grossmith in the lead, Ko-Ko. According to legend, one of the girls from the Japanese exhibition could only say 'sixpence please', which was the price of a cup of tea at the Knightsbridge exhibition. The style that successive generations of performers used in *The Mikado* dated back to this one girl.

Gilbert had also taken a slightly different approach to creating the opera; he had not begun with a plot. He had actually thought about creating roles for members of the company first, as he explained to the *New York Tribune* in 1885:

The original three little maids from school, 1885; Sybil Grey, Leonora Braham and Jessie Bond.

'The accident that Miss Braham, Miss Jessie Bond, and Miss Sybil Grey, are short in stature and all of a height, suggested the advisability of grouping them as three Japanese schoolgirls who should work together throughout the piece [*Three Little Maids from School*]. The next thing was to decide upon two scenes, which should be characteristic and effective. The respective advantages of a street in Nagasaki, a Japanese market-place, a wharf with shipping, a Japanese garden, a seaside beach, and the courtyard of a Japanese palace, were duly weighed; and the courtyard and the Japanese garden were finally decided upon.'

Just four days before Christmas, Sullivan wrote the first piece of music for the new opera; *Three Little Maids from School Are We*. There was also the question of language. For a time there was a popularly held myth that some of the words were in fact foul language in Japanese, but this was not in fact true. *The Mikado* was actually banned in 1907. According to Arthur Diósy, who was a respected traveller, lecturer and writer of Japanese and Far Eastern subjects and was quoted in *The Globe* newspaper:

'[He] says that it was at the suggestion of Mr Richard Temple, the original Mikado in the opera, that he himself supplied Sir Arthur with some real Japanese music in this particular tune, a famous Japanese war march. [He] points out that the story of the opera is entirely fantastic, having nothing Japanese in it, except the name of the Lord High Executioner, Ko-Ko, which means pickles.'

The Times reviewed *The Mikado* on Monday, March 16, 1885:

'After the production of *Princess Ida* rumour would have it that the joint authors, Mr. Gilbert and Sir Arthur Sullivan were alive to the necessity of turning over, as it were, a new leaf, and that their next venture would be of a different type: less farcical, more psychologically subtle, more serious in fact, albeit still humorous. There was a certain amount unfairness, not to say ingratitude for much harmless amusement received in such a supposition. A writer and a composer generally know best what they can do best, both conjointly and separately; and it may be safely assumed that, if Mr.

Gilbert and Sir Arthur Sullivan thought their united strength to lie in serious or even serio-comic work, they would have undertaken such work long before a certain feeling of monotony and tedium had begun to attach to their concetti and verbal quibbles and pretty tunes.

However this may be, certain it is that *The Mikado*, the new operetta produced at the Savoy Theatre on Saturday evening, does not in any marked degree differ from its numerous predecessors. All the elements which have gone to the making of many successes, and which by this time might be expressed by a mathematical formula of a+b-c without a single unknown quantity of x or y in the equation, are present. We have a comic monarch and a "bloated oligarch", and no end of Court officials and simpering maidens, whose little life is rounded by the vision of a handsome lover and a becoming frock. These people sing sentimental and comic ditties, and "patter songs" with "topical" allusions to the Japanese village in Knightsbridge and the present Ministry, after the approved fashion; they likewise ogle and flirt and attitudinize, and Mr. Grossmith dances a breakdown. The characters, or at least the types of the drama, are the same although they wear their clothes with a difference.

The robes of the British peers in *Iolanthe* have been exchanged for the flowing draperies of Daimios, the academic gowns of Princess Ida's fellow-collegiates have been laid aside for tight skirts, long sleeves, and the curious bustle which, by the way, is in reality a shawl which Japanese ladies unfold and sit upon when so inclined. Let it be acknowledged at once that these dresses are as gorgeous and exquisitely coloured as they are scrupulously correct, that they are worn, moreover, by the actors and actresses with an ease and propriety little short of marvellous. Mr. Grossmith and Mr. Barrington walk and sit as if petticoats had been their ordinary garb from infancy; and Miss Braham, Miss Jessie Bond, and Miss Sybil Grey flirt their fan, and walk with their feet turned in and look so charming withal, that their equals would with difficulty be found on fans or screens or in real life. It is curious, moreover, to see the old adage that the coat makes the man verified in so striking a manner. The European physiognomy marvellously adapts itself to the changed conditions of hair and head-dress, and seen from some distance and in the deceptive light of the stage the English counterfeit at the Savoy is scarcely distinguishable from the genuine article at the Japanese village. For this reason alone the student of comparative ethnology should pay a visit to both exhibitions. The lover of picturesque grouping and harmonious Eastern colour need not be exhorted to do the same.

It is a pity that the illusion thus carefully prepared by the costumier and the scene painter is not in any sense kept up by the author. No attempt has been made to mingle the slightest infusion of Eastern imagery or quaintness with the dialogue or the lyrics, which run throughout in the well-worn grooves of burlesque. Much additional fun might have been derived from such intermixture, which Mr. Gilbert would have been quite capable of accomplishing if so minded. He has, however, preferred not to tax the perception of his admirers by new ingredients, and the composer has followed his example. Sir Arthur Sullivan ignores the pentatonic scale and the minor keys (without a leading note) affected by the musicians of Japan; neither does he treat us to a solo on the 13-stringed dulcimer, called Sé by the Chinese and Koto by the Japanese. There is, it is true, a march prominently used in the overture and afterwards sung by the chorus when the Mikado enters in state. The motive of the theme is presumably genuine, but the treatment and instrumentation are essentially Western and modern. Perhaps the composer – as, indeed, the author – has acted wisely in eschewing novelty of invention or colouring. There were, perhaps, not 30 persons among the audience who had so much as heard about a pentatonic scale or a koto; while the familiar tunes, given in abundance, every one can remember, and whistle, and play, too, when the pianoforte score appears in due course. In burlesque opera familiarity does not breed contempt; rather the reverse.

The story on which Mr. Gilbert's libretto is founded is extremely slight, and, if the truth must be owned, so childish that on being compelled to sum it up on paper one blushes at the remembrance of many a hearty laugh it has excited. The Mikado, a highly moral sovereign, has, it appears, issued a decree condemning to death every man found guilty of flirtation "unless connubially linked". To evade this stern sentence the citizens of Titipu have hit upon the idea explained in the following lines:–

'And so we straight let out on bail
A convict from the county jail
Whose head was next
On some pretext
Condemnèd to be mown off,
And made him Headsman, for we said,
"Who's next to be decapited
Cannot cut off another's head
Until he's cut his own off."'

A Chicago poster featuring Nanki-Poo from The Mikado *dated 1885.* From the Library of Congress collection.

The person thus raised to the exalted dignity of Lord High Executioner is Ko-Ko, the cheap tailor (Mr. Grossmith), and, to crown his happiness, he is about to be married to his lovely ward, Yum-Yum by name (Miss Braham). This prospective bliss is disturbed, however, by a letter from the Mikado, who, struck by the fact that no executions have taken place at Titipu for a year, decrees that, unless somebody is beheaded within the space of one month, the office of Lord High Executioner shall be abolished and the city reduced to the rank of a village. Ko-Ko, who is first on the condemned list, naturally objects to committing self-execution, which, as he remarks, is a capital offence.

Fortunately, a substitute is found in the person of Nanki-Poo (Mr. Lely), a wandering minstrel, who loves Yum-Yum and agrees to be beheaded at the end of one mouth, provided he be allowed to marry her for that month. "My position during the next month will be most unpleasant," Ko-Ko remarks; "but, dear me! after all it is only putting off my wedding for a month," he philosophically adds.

At the marriage feast which is accordingly prepared a new complication arises in the shape of Katisha (Miss Rosina Brandram), a very formidable virago, and the daughter-in-law elect of the Mikado. Nanki-Poo is the son of that monarch, and it was to escape wedlock with Katisha that he fled from his father's Court and assumed the disguise of a musician. This, the lady explains, or rather tries to explain, for the excited guests will not admit her to audible speech.

In the second act the Mikado (Mr. R. Temple) appears on the scene to look after his fugitive son and heir. Ko-Ko, who believes that his imperial master is intent upon witnessing the long-delayed execution, forges an affidavit to the effect that Nanki-Poo has been beheaded that morning, being aided and abetted in his falsehood by Pooh-Bah, a great nobleman, who, in spite of his ancestors, has consented to serve under the ci-devant chief tailor in the manifold capacities of First Lord of the Treasury, Lord Chief Justice, Commander-in-Chief, Archbishop of Titipu, and Lord Mayor, and further castigates his family pride by accepting miscellaneous bribes from any one inclined to pay. This character has really little to do with the action, but, played as it is with the perfection of stolid humour by Mr. Rutland Barrington, it greatly adds to the general effect. The horror of Ko-Ko may be imagined when it is discovered that the wandering minstrel whom he pretends to have beheaded is the Crown Prince of Japan. That Prince, moreover, declines to reappear in the land of the living as long as the formidable Katisha remains single.

Finally Ko-Ko reluctantly makes up his mind to marry the lady himself, and this obstacle being removed all ends happily. It is scarcely necessary to add that this thread of story is eked out and diversified by the quaint entanglements of Mr. Gilbert's humour. Here is an instance of that humour at its best:–

"Nanki-Poo (about to betray his exalted identity). – But (aside), shall I tell her? Yes. She will not betray me. (Aloud.) What if it should prove after all that I am no musician.

"Yum-Yum. – There! I was certain of it the moment I heard you play."

And, again, where Katisha, conscious of her super-annuated charms, describes herself as "an acquired taste." In other places the line between genuine fun and a mere tickling of the ears of the groundlings is not sufficiently observed, as, for example, where the same lady, speaking of the irresistible fascination of her right elbow, adds, "It is on view Tuesdays and Fridays on presentation of visiting card." This is far-fetched and common at the same time.

The position of Sir Arthur Sullivan in this, as in many a previous operetta, reminds one of that of a hero and a martyr, braving dangers and overcoming difficulties at which a less skilful and perhaps more fastidious musician would stand aghast. To write music in the least relevant to such verses as those above quoted one would think impossible were not the established fact before one's eyes. And yet the composer does not only this, but he actually adds points to the humour of those verses, as, for example, by means of the orchestral wails which accompany the sensational story of the mock trial already referred to. As another among many instances of genuine vis comica we may cite a trio for male voices towards the end of the first act. That in other places the ingenuity even of Sir Arthur Sullivan fails to establish any rapport between music and words is not a matter for surprise.

The most ambitious number of the score is at the end of the first act, a very long piece, designed on the model of the orthodox operatic finale. It is, however, less successful than similar efforts from the same pen. The melodious development is not sufficiently broad for the purpose it has to serve, and the entire design lacks coherence till the beginning of Katisha's song, "The hour of gladness," after which an excellent dramatic climax is attained. For sentimental songs proper there is little opportunity, and the best specimen of this kind, "Hearts do not break," is curiously enough assigned to the forbidding Katisha. Very graceful is the female chorus and trio, "Comes a train of little ladies" in the first act, while the duet between Yum-Yum and her lover, which follows soon after, is, by way of contrast, as feeble as can well be imagined. The inevitable "old English" madrigal (sung by Japanese!) is not wanting.

To sum up, *The Mikado* is likely to hold its own among the series of pretty and enjoyable operettas which we owe to Mr. Gilbert and Sir Arthur Sullivan. As a piece of stage show it is, perhaps, the best of all. In a dramatic and musical sense it holds a medium position, being scarcely as good as *The Sorcerer* and The Pinafore, and certainly infinitely better than *Iolanthe* or *Princess Ida*.

Of the performance we can very concisely speak, because it was as near perfection as a first performance can be. The principal artists, with the exception of Mr. Bovill (Pish-Tush, an irrelevant noble), have already been named. All did well in parts specially adapted to the qualities as actors and singers of which they have shown themselves possessed in other characters of a similar type. Thanks to the author and composer, the ensemble was without flaw or hesitation.

As to the success of the piece there can be no doubt after its reception on Saturday night. Moreover, the popularity of the two collaborators has reached the point where success depends no longer on intrinsic merit. They resemble the poet in the famous parable, which, being told indifferently of Japan and China, may fitly conclude this notice of a Japanese opera. Huang Lu, so says the Chinese version of the tale, was the greatest poet and musician ever born. His verses were replete with wisdom and sweetness, and when he sang the stars stood still in their courses. When he died his gentle craft passed by some miraculous process into the golden pen he had used; unfortunately, after some generations that pen was lost. Many years later a mediocre rhymester had occasion to do an important service to a fairy, and as his reward asked for the pen of Huang Lu. This, or rather the loan of this, the fairy procured for him for five years. His verses during that time were replete with wisdom and sweetness, and he became as famous almost as Huang Lu himself. When at the end of five years the fairy claimed the pen the door poetaster was in despair, but his benefactress said "Be comforted, for henceforth it matters not what you write. The Chinese public will accept anything from you." So will the English public up to a certain point.'

The Mikado's original length of run was 672 performances. It was in two acts and billed as an original Japanese opera, with the subtitle *The Town of Titipu*.

The Mikado Cast and Synopsis

The Mikado of Japan	Richard Temple
Nanki-Poo	Derward Lely
Ko-Ko	George Grossmith
Pooh-Bah	Rutland Barrington
Pish-Tush	Frederick Bovill
Yum-Yum	Leonora Braham
Pitti-Sing	Jessie Bond
Peep-Bo	Sybil Grey
Katisha	Rosina Brandram

Act I

A wandering minstrel, Nanki-Poo, approaches a group of men in Titipu and asks them whether they know where the ward of the tailor Ko-Ko, Yum-Yum might be. The minstrel is in love with Yum-Yum, but after she became engaged to Ko-Ko Nanki-Poo left Titipu a broken man. He discovers that Ko-Ko has been condemned to death and Nanki-Poo wants to find Yum-Yum. One of the lords tells him that Ko-Ko is no longer in prison but is in fact the Lord High Executioner. Ko-Ko had

A Chicago poster, probably 1885, for The Mikado. From the Library of Congress collection.

been put in prison for flirting and now he is in this powerful position he is seeking to change the laws. Nanki-Poo is told by Pooh-Bah that the wedding preparations are well underway. Yum-Yum and her two sisters return from school and she meets Nanki-Poo. He tells her that he is in fact the son of the Mikado and that his father has ordered him to marry Katisha, an elderly lady attached to the court. Ko-Ko receives a letter from the Mikado and he demands an execution within a month, so a victim needs to be found. Nanki-Poo is so distraught that he is contemplating suicide, making an ideal candidate for execution. Nanki-Poo agrees to be executed if he is allowed to marry Yum-Yum. Katisha now arrives and tries to tell everyone that Nanki-Poo is the Mikado's son.

Act II

Nanki-Poo and Yum-Yum marry. What neither of them realised is that if the husband is executed then the wife has to be buried alive. Nanki-Poo offers to commit suicide to avoid this fate for Yum-Yum. Ko-Ko is also in a quandary; on the one hand he has never executed anyone before and is frightened, but he is also terrified to incur the wrath of the Mikado. It is decided to fake the execution. The Mikado now arrives and Ko-Ko tells him that the execution has already taken place. The two lovers have in fact run away. The Mikado falls for the ruse and then tells Ko-Ko that he is in fact looking for his son. It then dawns on the Mikado that the man that Ko-Ko has supposedly executed was in fact his own son and therefore Ko-Ko, Pooh-Bah and Pitti-Sing must be executed for killing the heir to the throne. Nanki-Poo declares that he will not show himself until Kathisa is engaged to someone else and has no longer any claim on him. Ko-Ko proceeds to woe her, which allows Nanki-Poo to reappear. Ko-Ko must now face a future with an angry Katisha, who he has deceived.

Both the critics and the audiences adored *The Mikado*. Sullivan wrote in his diary on March 14, 1885:

> 'A most brilliant house. Tremendous reception. All went well except Grossmith whose nervousness nearly upset the piece. A treble encore for *Three Little Maids* and *The Flowers that Bloom in the Spring*. Seven encores taken – might have been twelve.'

The critics were especially enthusiastic, variously describing it as 'fresh', 'brilliant', 'captivating' and 'splendidly displayed'.

The Mikado would become their biggest hit, but there was another major row brewing with D'Oyly Carte. D'Oyly Carte, according to their agreement, would hold the preliminary auditions. He would choose the chorus and understudies. Gilbert and Sullivan had a veto and they always chose the principal performers. They controlled rehearsals, but after first night the maintenance of standards was down to D'Oyly Carte. He paid the cast, stage staff, organised advertising, bought equipment and generally maintained the theatre.

Gilbert in particular thought that D'Oyly Carte had too much power and wrote to him:

'It seems to me that we are not all of the same opinion as to our respective positions under the contract framed some time ago.'

D'Oyly Carte replied:

'I cannot see how you and Sullivan are part managers of the theatre, any more than I am part-author or part-composer of the music.'

Angered beyond measure, Gilbert wrote back on June 1, 1885:

'I am at a loss to express the pain and surprise with which I read your letter. As you decline to permit me to have any voice in the control of the theatre that Sullivan and I have raised to its present position of prosperity and distinction, and point out to me that, by our agreement, I am merely a hack author employed by you to supply you with pieces on certain terms, I have no alternative but to accept the position you assign to me during the few months that our agreement has got to run. Henceforth I will be bound by its absolute and literal terms. If this course of action should result in inconvenience or loss to yourself you will do me the justice to remember that this is of your own creation.'

D'Oyly Carte replied in conciliatory terms:

'Your note grieves me more than I can say. Must a dramatic author be considered a hack author if he does not arrange the number of stalls in the theatre where his opera is played? What is my position compared to yours? I envy your position, but I could never attain it. If I could be an author like you I would certainly not be a manager. I am simply the tradesman who sells your creations of art.'

Gilbert was quite adamant about wanting a share in the management of the theatre and he was also concerned that D'Oyly Carte might make the wrong decisions and bring ruin to them all. D'Oyly Carte told them that it was not just the Savoy to worry about; there were up to six provincial tours, plus the work in America and Australia. He warned that if they were to be consulted on everything then they would have no time for anything else.

An 1885 cartoon by Alfred Bryan depicting Gilbert in a suit of armour, with a mallet labelled 'discipline' and towering over the diminutive figures of Richard D'Oyly Carte.

The Ironmaster at the Savoy.

Sullivan stayed out of the dispute as best he could; in fact he was content with how things were. What had not helped, as far as Gilbert was concerned, was that Sullivan's contribution to the partnership was obviously valued far more highly by some than his own. A typical example was comments made in the *Daily Telegraph*:

'The beautiful things in *The Mikado* come when the composer appeals rather to tears than to laughter. Perhaps the oddest thing about this very odd opera that one of the most popular numbers in it is this beautiful madrigal which belongs to the English village green rather than the oriental garden, and in which Gilbert ceases to be the clown and writes quite seriously and finds an answering note in Sullivan's love and understanding of the idiom of seventeenth century madrigal music. The result is an un-Japanese as could be imagined.'

The article then went on to note that the song *Tit Willow* bore a striking resemblance to something that had been written by the poet Nicholas Rowe (1674-1718).

Meanwhile, D'Oyly Carte was taking steps to try and stop pirate productions from being staged in the United States. One of the pirate management companies from America sent a spy to London. D'Oyly Carte now launched a pre-emptive strike, as a document from the D'Oyly Carte archives reveals:

'After the enormous success of the opera in London two American managers entered into treaty with Mr D'Oyly Carte for the production of the piece in New York. These were Mr Stetson, of Fifth Avenue Theatre, and Mr Duff of the Standard. R D'Oyly Carte finally closed with Mr Stetson, and, annoyed by the success of his rival, Mr Duff resolved to pirate the piece, and play it in New York in advance of Mr Carte and, in defiance of the author and composer. Then commenced a campaign between the English and American managers, Mr Carte had arranged to produce *The Mikado* at the Fifth Avenue Theatre about the middle of October; but when he ascertained that it was Mr Duff's intention to forestall him by beginning his unauthorised performance in August, Mr Carte decided to steal the march on his opponent by placing all possible impediments in the way of his carrying out the scheme, and by so arranging his own plans that the first performance of *The Mikado* which the New Yorkers witnessed should be the genuine and the authorised one. Mr Carte was well aware that if he openly made preparations to take his artists over to America, the fact would be at once cabled to Mr Duff in New York, who would then have about ten days start in bringing out the opera with his own company. It was obvious that the expedition, if undertaken at all, must be organised secretly.'

D'Oyly Carte organised an English touring company to be secretly sent to the United States and booked 50 passages on the Cunard line. He even went to the extent of booking the passages under assumed names, out of Liverpool.

Meanwhile, Duff had sent one of his men to Liberty's to buy up Japanese costumes. As soon as the store discovered that the agent had nothing to do with D'Oyly Carte they refused to do business with him. The agent then made for Paris, but D'Oyly Carte was ahead of the game and had already sent one of his own men to buy every Japanese costume he could find. Everyone was sworn to secrecy, as the incommunicado cast members slipped out of Liverpool, bound for the United States. Nothing was left to chance, as discovery could mean that Duff would get a drop on D'Oyly Carte.

As it turned out, *The Mikado* opened in Fifth Avenue Theatre on August 19 and ran for 430 performances. D'Oyly Carte had beaten Duff. But by the following year there were over 170 pirate versions of *The Mikado* being performed across America. D'Oyly Carte used law against them, with a test case in New York. The ruling was 'copyright, or no copyright, commercial honesty or commercial buccaneering, no Englishman possesses any rights which a true born American is bound to respect.'

Sullivan conducted a gala performance on September 24, 1885 in New York.

Ruddigore

In the period 1885 to 1887 Sullivan was the conductor of the Philharmonic Society in London. 1886 was to prove an exceptionally busy year, with Sullivan composing an oratorio, *The Golden Legend*, which was performed at the Leeds Festival. This relegated a new opera to a very poor second place. However the result was to be *Ruddigore*.

For inspiration Gilbert had returned to an earlier play, *Ages Ago*. Somehow Sullivan managed to complete the score around a week before the opening, on January 22, 1887. The subtitle of the opera was *The Witches Curse*.

The first night would be something of a flop and there was a mixture of cheers and boos at the end of the performance. For most it was nowhere near as good as *The Mikado*; it had one of the longest running first acts, at 88 minutes, and many thought that the second act dragged

The drawing of the Baronettes of Ruddigore, as they emerge from the picture frames. This is an engraving dated at around 1887.

and lacked direction. Gilbert and Sullivan responded by altering the second act and reducing its length. It actually ended up running longer than *Princess Ida*'s first run, at 288 nights. On opening night the queues for seats began just after noon and by six o'clock there were some 2,000 people waiting outside the theatre. There was also a last minute change in the title. Originally it had been called *Ruddygore* prompting people to call it 'bloodygore' so Gilbert changed it to *Ruddigore*.

Within days of its opening George Grossmith, who appeared as Robin Oakapple, had to have an operation for peritonitis. He was replaced by Henry Lytton, who would later write:

'Upon the Monday morning I was told I was to play the part – and play it that very night. Then the cue came and I went on. The silence of the audience was deathly. They gave me not the slightest welcome. The great Grossmith, the lion comique of his day, was not playing. Robin Oakapple was being taken by an unknown stripling. No wonder they were disappointed and chilling. First I had a few lines to speak and then I had a beautiful little duet with Miss Leonora Braham who was playing Rose Maybud. And when that duet *Poor Little Man* was over, and we had responded to the calls for an encore, all my tremors and hesitation had gone. I knew things were all right. The applause when the curtain fell was to be unforgettable. It betokened a triumph.'

This review appeared in the *Illustrated London News* on January 29, 1887:

'The specialty of last week was the new comic opera written by Mr. W. S. Gilbert, and composed by Sir Arthur Sullivan – a piece from their associated genius being an event of equal dramatic and musical interest; the great and deserved success of their several previous works of the kind having induced eager expectation for any new essay. The co-operation of the two gentlemen referred to

The original Ruddigore, *from* The Illustrated Sporting and Dramatic News, *1887.*

has been a happy coincidence, similar to that of the united labours of Scribe and Auber in their delightful works of the opera-comique class.

The production of "Ruddygore, or the Witch's Curse" is noticed in the theatrical column of this week, and it is, therefore, only necessary here to refer briefly to the musical interest of the piece, which is quite equal to that of its predecessors from the same hands. The vocal score will not be published for some weeks to come, when we shall be able to refer again to its merits; meantime, we may point to some of the pieces that proved attractive in performance, and will doubtless be permanently popular. Rose Maybud's expressive ballad, "If somebody there chance to be"; the piquant duet, "I know a youth", for her and Robin Oakapple; Richard Dauntless's robust nautical ballad, "I've shipped, d'ye see, in a Revenue sloop" (with its capital hornpipe climax); the suave love duet, "The battle's roar is over", for this character and Rose; the spirited trio, "In sailing o'er life's ocean", for the personages already named; Mad Margaret's scene, and ballad, "To a garden"; Sir Despard Murgatroyd's sententious solo, "Oh, why am I moody" (with its interspersed choral comments); the impulsive duet, "You understand" for him and Richard, the beautiful madrigal, and the several movements which close the first act are all effective in their respective styles.

In the second (and last) act, the music in the scene of the animation of the portraits in the picture gallery is highly dramatic in its appropriate sombreness of style and impressive orchestral effects. This is preceded by a pretty duet (with chorus), "Happily coupled" – for Rose and Richard; and a refined ballad, "In bygone days", for the former. Sir Roderic Murgatroyd's sombre song, "When the night-wind howls" – with the surrounding choral and orchestral accessories – rises to a dramatic and musical height worthy of grand opera; and throws into strong relief the exquisitely quaint music of the subsequent duet, "I once was a very abandoned person", for Sir Despard and Margaret in their ludicrously altered aspects. The patter trio for these two and Robin; Hannah's sentimental ballad, "There grew a little flower"; and a well-contrasted finale are prominent features of the closing division of the work. The principal performers have been as well fitted with their music as with their dramatic characters, the performance of which is noted in our article, "The Playhouses"; and it must here be said that Misses Braham, Bond, and Brandram, and Messrs. G. Grossmith, D. Lely, R. Barrington, R. Temple, and others, worthily fulfilled the vocal requirements.

There is some bright and tuneful music for female chorus in each act; and the orchestral details, throughout, are rich in colouring and variety of detail. As in his other productions of the same class, Sir Arthur Sullivan has eminently succeeded alike in the expression of refined sentiment and comic humour. In the former respect, the charm of graceful melody prevails; while, in the latter, the music of the most grotesque situations is redolent of fun, without the slightest approach to vulgarity or coarseness – in this

Rutland Barrington as Sir Despard Murgatroyd and Jessie Bond as Mad Margaret in Ruddigore.

113

latter respect, how unlike some of the French buffo music of the day! The composer conducted the performance on the first night, using, in the scene of darkness (in the second act), a baton illuminated by the electric light.'

It was originally billed as a new and original supernatural opera in two acts. The first act was set in a fishing village in Cornwall and the second in Ruddigore Castle.

Ruddigore Cast and Synopsis

Sir Ruthven Murgatroyd (Robin Oakapple)	George Grossmith
Richard Dauntless	Derward Lely
Sir Despard Murgatroyd	Rutland Barrington
Old Adam Goodheart	Rudolph Lewis
Rose Maybud	Leonora Braham
Mad Margaret	Jessie Bond
Dame Hannah	Rosina Brandram
Zorah	Josephine Findlay
Ruth	Miss Lindsay
Sir Rupert Murgatroyd	Sidney Price
Sir Jasper Murgatroyd	Harold or Percy Charles
Sir Lionel Murgatroyd	Harris Trevor
Sir Conrad Murgatroyd	Percy Burbank
Sir Desmond Murgatroyd	Mr Tuer
Sir Gilbert Murgatroyd	James Wilbraham
Sir Mervin Murgatroyd	Mr Cox
Sir Roderic Murgatroyd	Richard Temple

Act I

Rose Maybud does not wish to get married, which leaves a group of professional bridesmaids out of work in the village of Rederring in Cornwall. Dame Hannah is asked to marry simply to give them some work. She tells of how a witch was burned on the village green and had brought a curse to the baronets of Ruddigore. One of the baronets had been Hannah's suitor and the curse meant that the baronets would have to commit a crime every day, or die. Robin Oakapple, who is a young farmer, loves Rose Maybud and she loves him, but will not admit it. Robin Oakapple is really the true baronet of Ruddigore and he will not take his title because he will then be subject to the curse. Robin's half-brother, Richard Dauntless, knows the truth; he is a sailor who has just returned from a voyage. Richard determines to talk to Rose on Robin's behalf but he falls in love with her and they are discovered by Robin and the bridesmaids. When Rose realises that Robin loves her she turns Richard down. Mad Margaret has been driven into madness because of her love for Sir Despard Murgatroyd. He is Robin's younger brother and is the baronet of Ruddigore, only because he believes Robin to be dead. When Richard appears Robin tells him the truth. Rose and Robin are to be wed, but Sir Despard claims Robin and announces him to be the true heir to Ruddigore and the curse. Robin leaves and Richard consoles Rose, whilst Sir Despard talks to Mad Margaret.

Act II

Robin and his servant, Adam Goodheart, are now in Ruddigore Castle. Robin wants out of the curse and appeals to his ancestors. Their ghostly forms appear. Sir Roderic demands to hear which crimes Robin has committed, but he is unimpressed. The ghosts tell Robin that he needs to kidnap a woman or he will perish. Robin sends Adam to carry out the kidnapping. Meanwhile, Sir Despard and Margaret arrive; they have rekindled their relationship and tell Robin to defy the ancestors and suffer the consequences. Robin has forgotten that he has sent Adam out to kidnap a woman and Adam returns with Dame Hannah. Sir Roderic recognises Dame Hannah as his lover. Suddenly Robin realises that there is a way out; as the baronet he will die by refusing to commit a crime everyday and if he does so it is the same as committing suicide, which is a crime. So in fact none of the baronets had to die in the first place; this lifts the curse. Rose now has Robin, Roderic has Dame Hannah and Richard plumps for Zorah, the chief bridesmaid, thus providing work for all of the professional bridesmaids.

In truth, by this stage, Sullivan was completely bored and disheartened by the operas and derived far more pleasure and critical acclaim, as far as he was concerned, for his more 'serious' music. He was asked by the Prince of Wales to compose an ode to celebrate Queen Victoria's jubilee.

No sooner had he begun work on it than Gilbert wrote to him, suggesting that they meet.

Ruddigore had finished its run at the Savoy in 1887 and all three of the partners were downhearted. As a stopgap measure *HMS Pinafore* was revived. For some time Gilbert had been trying to foist his so-called lozenge plot on Sullivan. In effect, it meant some lozenge; potion or talisman would make people act in odd or strange ways. The problem with the lozenge plot was that it was predictable and it had been used in *The Sorcerer*.

Once again Sullivan rejected the idea, but the situation was saved; Gilbert was waiting for a train at Uxbridge station and he saw a beefeater standing against the background of the Tower of London. It was an advertisement for the Tower Furnishing Company. Gilbert later wrote:

'I thought the beefeater would make a good picturesque central figure for another Savoy opera and my intention was to give it a modern setting, with the characteristics and development of burlesque – to make it another Sorcerer. But then I decided to make it a romantic and dramatic piece, and to put it back into Elizabethan times.'

In Sullivan's diary on Christmas Day 1887 his reaction to it was clear:

'Gilbert read the plot of the new piece [*The Tower of London*]: immensely pleased with it. Pretty story, no topsy-turvydom, very human and funny also.'

In fact the opera's name would change several times, from *The Tower of London* to the *Tower Warder* to *The Beefeaters* and then finally to *The Yeoman of the Guard*.

Sullivan's ink was scarcely dry when it was handed over, even up to the final rehearsal. There had been arguments between Gilbert and Sullivan throughout and there were major production problems up until the last minute. Once again Gilbert had worked hard to get the look of the opera right; he had visited the Tower of London on numerous occasions and taken sketches of the warders. He even provided Sullivan with alternative versions of the lyrics. There was also a major problem with the title; in fact the Yeoman of the Guard are not the warders of the Tower of

London, but the monarch's personal bodyguard. But none of this seemed to matter at the time.

Meanwhile, Alfred Cellier, who had been a conductor of some of the earlier Gilbert and Sullivan operas, was gaining popularity as a composer of comic operas himself. This was of considerable concern to Gilbert and Sullivan; they now had a major competitor. Cellier's *Dorothy* was being performed at the Gaiety Theatre and closed after 931 shows; something that had not so far been achieved by Gilbert and Sullivan. D'Oyly Carte was also considering moving in a different direction and was contemplating building a large theatre to put on English operas.

The Yeoman of the Guard

The Yeoman of the Guard opened on October 3, 1888. Gilbert was especially nervous on the first night, but the audiences loved it and it ran for 423 performances. *The Times* reviewed the performance of Thursday, October 4, 1888:

> '*In The Yeomen of the Guard*, the latest operetta by Mr. Gilbert and Sir Arthur Sullivan, produced at the Savoy Theatre last night, the author and to some extent the composer have, in familiar phrase, turned over a new leaf. Whether Mr. Gilbert felt that a vein of very original but not very profound humour had been thoroughly worked out – whether the comparatively small success of *Ruddigore* had been accepted as a warning that the public required a change – certain it is that *The Yeomen of the Guard* differs from its numerous predecessors in many important respects. The quaint and whimsical medium through which Mr. Gilbert looks upon men and things has been known to his numerous admirers ever since the inimitable "Bab Ballads," of which these operettas are essentially an amplified and dramatized development, were given to the world. His startling paradoxes, his twists of character, his new versions and perversions of familiar relations of life have given pleasure to thousands, and never more so than when they were accompanied by Sir Arthur Sullivan's pretty tunes.
>
> Of all this there is comparatively little in the libretto of the new piece. Here we have a serious plot of a romantic kind carried on in lively but rational dialogue of the Elizabethan pattern, the action

taking place in the 16th century, and the scene being laid on Tower-green, with the ancient Norman fortress frowning in the background. It is true that Mr. Grossmith varies the proceedings by sundry jeux de mots, "irritating" to one of the characters in the play, and perhaps to some among the audience. He also dances in conjunction with a comic gaoler the orthodox breakdown, and sings a "patter" song in which bishops and doctors of divinity are referred to in the most familiar manner and in language strangely out of keeping with the archaisms of the dialogue. But then Mr. Grossmith enacts the part of Point, a professional jester, and a professional jester in the Gilbertian order of things ought to be the most serious of the dramatis personæ.

The form of art here adopted is in brief essentially that generally described as "English opera," as developed by Balfe and Wallace, which form consists of spoken dialogue instead of recitative, and of a certain number of lyrics sung by the various characters at odd moments while the action is waiting. Only in the ensembles and finales is there any opportunity for the composer to take an integral part in the dramatic proceedings. It should, in the first instance, be acknowledged that Mr. Gilbert has earnestly endeavoured to leave familiar grooves and rise to higher things on his abandoned self as on stepping stones. Whether the move in the new direction will be altogether a successful one is a different question, which at present it would be premature to decide. The effect on last night's very friendly audience was an interesting psychological study. When in one of these operettas a grave-looking elder speaks this wise – "No, my lass; but there's one hope yet. Thy brother Leonard, who, as a reward for his valour in saving his standard and cutting his way through 50 foes who would have hanged him, has been appointed Yeoman of the Guard" – every one expects, and the audience expected last night, that the elder would presently do or say something outrageously comic, and that Leonard would turn out a coward. When neither turned out to be the case the spectators were evidently a little doubtful whether to take everything au sérieux or to titter in advance at some joke which sometimes failed to come.

In the midst of this the downright fun of Mr. Grossmith was almost a relief. Here the audience were on familiar ground, and enjoyed themselves accordingly. The patter song was applauded to the echo, and the duet with Wilfred Shadbolt, the comical gaoler, followed by the breakdown already referred to, was received with a roar of laughter, not perhaps quite agreeable to the author in the circumstances. Let it not, however, be supposed that the new piece lacks brightness and merriment. There are some pretty and well-arranged dances; the costumes, including a splendid array of beefeaters, are tasteful and historically appropriate, and even sensation is represented in the shape of the headsman carrying his axe, and with a black mask on his face.

Moreover, there is the music. Whatever may be thought of the new piece, it has undoubtedly the merit of having given an excellent chance to the composer; the fact of the action taking place in England would be sufficient to establish the point. Sir Arthur Sullivan, as we have frequently said, is among our modern school of musicians the foremost, perhaps the only prominent, composer who is essentially English. The forms of early English music – the madrigal, the part-song, the glee – are as a second nature to him, and he produces their modern counterparts with a freedom and a faithfulness which alone would account for his unrivalled popularity. Even in a Japanese opera these features were appreciated; but here, being eminently suited to the action, they are simply invaluable. It is true that some of the soli partake of the modern drawing-room ballad rather than of the early English song of Purcell and of Henry Lawes, Milton's friend, which was essentially of a declamatory character. Thus the song, "When our gallant Norman foes," admirably sung by Miss Rosina Brandram, which is obviously intended to redeem the insignificant part of Dame Carruthers, is not as quaint as might be, and the tenor air in the second act, "Free from his fetters grim," is downright commonplace; but what, on the other hand, can be more charming than the ditty with whichMiss Jessie Bond, a winsome Ph?be, opens the play, or the duet, "I have a song to sing, O!" in which Miss Geraldine Ulmar and Mr. Grossmith join their voices, and finally the unaccompanied four-part song, "Strange adventure," a perfect gem of its kind, in which the sympathetic soprano of Miss Kate Hervey (sic. Rose Hervey – ed.) as a nondescript niece told admirably?

The general type of Sir Arthur Sullivan's music is a kind of happy mean between the earlier style of his operettas and that here adopted. Sometimes the two appear in close juxtaposition. Thus the recitative passages beginning "Leonard, I beg your pardon?" are cast in the mould of opéra comique, while the trio which ensues belongs unmistakably to opéra bouffe. Inequalities of treatment occur almost of necessity. In Elsie's ballad the note of mixed sentiment and humour which inspired the charming words is scarcely struck by the music, while in the ballad sung by Ph?be immediately afterwards verse and tune are perfectly blended. Among concerted pieces we may specially mention the song of the Yeomen, forming a kind of canto fermo to the graceful arabesques of the female voices in the first act, and the finale of the same act, which recalls to mind similar ensembles in The Sorcerer, minus of course the mock-heroic element, which would be out of place here. To sum up, Sir Arthur Sullivan's score is fully equal to previous achievements and the success of the piece will no doubt be largely due to it.

The plot may be summed up in a few words. Colonel Fairfax (Mr. Courtice Pounds) is imprisoned in the Tower and condemned to death on a charge of witchcraft. Fortunately for himself, he has on a previous occasion saved the life of Sergeant Meryll, of the Yeomen of the Guard (Mr. Richard Temple), and that worthy soldier, together with his pretty daughter, Phoebe (Miss Jessie Bond), resolve upon a rescue. The Sergeant's son is about to return from the wars, and his place as one of the Beefeaters is assumed by Colonel Fairfax, who manages to escape from his cell by the aid of Phoebe, that damsel having by stealth obtained the keys from her admirer, Wilfred Shadbolt, the head gaoler (Mr. W. H. Denny). In the meanwhile, however, a new complication has arisen. To defeat the design on his property of a wicked relative, Colonel Fairfax has asked and obtained permission to contract a marriage just before his execution, and Elsie Maynard (Miss Geraldine Ulmar), a strolling singer, has for the sum of 100 crowns consented to be his wife and widow within an hour. During the ceremony, which is supposed to take place behind the scenes, both are for some occult reason blindfolded, and therefore do not know each other when they meet again on Tower-green after the Colonel has been enrolled among the Yeomen. As a matter of course they fall in love with each other, and when, equally as a matter of course, the Colonel's pardon arrives and he throws off his disguise, they are only too happy to be man and wife.

The incident of the marriage before execution is generally familiar from the French play in which Frédéric Lemaître acted Don Cæsar de Bazan, and from its operatic offspring, Wallace's Maritana, where, by the way, the reason for blindfolding the gentleman as well as the lady is fully explained. So obvious, indeed, is the resemblance that one would be inclined to suspect some subtle attempt at parody, did not the serious tone of Mr. Gilbert's work preclude any such thought.

Of the performance we need not speak in detail, not at least as far as the old members of the Savoy company are concerned. Every one knows that such artists as Miss Jessie Bond, Miss Brandram, Mr. Grossmith, and Mr. Richard Temple have fully entered into Mr. Gilbert's spirit and act every part, be it Japanese maid from school, or pirate of Penzance, or sorcerer, exactly as he wishes and has taught them to act it. Miss Geraldine Ulmar will have to moderate her powerful voice in the ensembles and tone down her action before she can be said to fit perfectly in the general picture. There were two new-comers in the cast, both of whom must be called decided acquisitions. Mr. C. Pounds, the Colonel Fairfax of the evening, is a better actor and a better tenor than any of his predecessors, and his conception of the part of the 16th century gallant, including a slight exaggeration of gesture, was intelligent throughout. As regards singing, he should practise the voce di peto. To Mr. Denny had fallen the difficult task of creating the part of the gaoler, obviously designed for Mr. Rutland Barrington, who has left the Savoy Theatre. That the new actor was quite equal to his inimitable prototype cannot be said, but he showed considerable humour of the dry kind nevertheless.

The reception of the piece was all that the warmest admirers of author and composer could have desired. Many songs were encored, and of some, as, for example, the duet of Elsie and Point, with its quaint accompaniment of the hurdy-gurdy type, the audience seemed never to tire. Of the weakness of the plot no one seemed to take notice in the excitement of the general success. Upon the whole we can agree with the popular verdict. Mr. Gilbert is in his way a man of genius, and even at his worst is a head and shoulders above the ordinary librettist. In the present instance he has not written a good play, but his lyrics are suave and good to sing, and, wedded to Sir Arthur Sullivan's melodies, they will no doubt find their way to many a home where English song is appreciated.'

This would be one of the operas that would barely be out of the D'Oyly Carte repertoire. There were numerous revivals, until the demise of the original D'Oyly Carte Company in 1982.

The Yeoman of the Guard Cast and Synopsis

Sir Richard Cholmondeley	Wallace Brownlow
Colonel Fairfax	Courtice Pounds
Sergeant Meryll	Richard Temple
Leonard Meryll	W R Shirley
Jack Point	George Grossmith
Wilfred Shadbolt	W H Denny
Headsman	H Richards
First Yeoman	James Wilbraham
Second Yeoman	Antonio Medcalf
Third Yeoman	Mr Merton
Fourth Yeoman	Rudolph Lewis
First citizen	Tom Redmond
Second citizen	Mr Boyd
Elsie Maynard	Geraldine Ulmar
Phoebe Meryll	Jessie Bond
Dame Caruthers	Rosina Brandram
Kate	Rose Hervey

Act I

Colonel Fairfax is due for execution and Phoebe Meryll sits alone on Tower Green. Her father, Sergeant Meryll, tells her that her brother Leonard is to be posted to the Tower as a warder. Both father and daughter hope that when he arrives he will bring with him a reprieve for Fairfax. In the event he does not and Sergeant Meryll comes up with the plan to free Fairfax and take the place of Leonard, who nobody else has seen as yet. Fairfax has been moved to the death cell, accused of sorcery. The accuser is a relative whose plan is to inherit his estate after he has been executed. Fairfax begs Sir Richard to find him a wife before he is executed, in order to thwart the inheritance expected by the evil relative. Two entertainers, Jack Point and Elsie Maynard, arrive at the Tower. They receive a very mixed reception from the audience, but Sir Richard reckons that Elsie would make a suitable wife for Fairfax. Elsie agrees and is led away blindfolded to the cell. She comes back a married woman. The Merylls now use Phoebe to distract the head jailer, Wilfred Shadbolt, in order to steal the key. She needs to play on his love for her so that her two relatives can take the key, open the door and then return the key without anyone being wiser. Fairfax now emerges, clean shaven and posing as Leonard. Three warders now go to Fairfax's cell, only to find it empty. Shadbolt is arrested and Jack Point and Elsie are horrified, as they now realise that Elsie's husband is not only still alive but also free.

Act II

Two days later and no one has managed to find Fairfax. Shadbolt and Jack Point come up with a scheme to claim that they have shot Fairfax and that he has fallen into the moat and sunk without trace. Fairfax discovers to his pleasure that Elsie is the woman that he married. He did not know, as she was still wearing a sack over her head. In his disguise Fairfax tries to woo Elsie, as does Jack Point. Fairfax wins. Shadbolt works out that Fairfax is posing as Leonard and in order to hide the secret Phoebe agrees to become engaged to Shadbolt. Leonard finally arrives with a reprieve for Fairfax, but a conversation between Meryll and Leonard is overheard by Dame Caruthers and Sergeant Meryll proposes to her to gain her silence. Elsie is overjoyed to discover that her husband is in fact Fairfax, the man that wooed her and that she fell in love with. Jack Point is distraught and senseless with grief at losing Elsie.

Both Gilbert and Sullivan were extremely happy with *The Yeoman of the Guard*, but they had not found it particularly easy to write. Gilbert had taken five months and Sullivan had to be very inventive. Both men considered it to be amongst the best work they had ever done together.

Individual work still continued, with Sullivan launching a revival of his fairy comedy, *The Wicked World*, for the first time in 15 years. This had opened on July 4, 1888 at the Savoy. After a Royal command performance of Sullivan's *The Golden Legend* at the Royal Albert Hall Queen Victoria had suggested to Sullivan that he write a grand opera.

One of the notable absentees from *The Yeoman of the Guard* was Rutland Barrington. He had decided to focus on stage play production and Gilbert had written *Brantinghame Hall*, which was performed at St James's Theatre.

By 1889 D'Oyly Carte was heavily involved in building a new theatre at the top of Shaftesbury Avenue. He called it the Royal English Opera

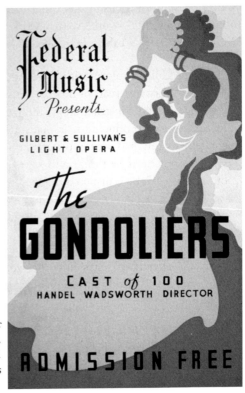

A poster for the Federal Music presentation of The Gondoliers, *created in either 1936 or 1937.* From the Library of Congress collection

House and asked Sullivan to write a grand opera for the opening night. Sullivan contacted Gilbert, but he took a realistic view, stating that he could probably not do his best work, as comic operas were his forte. Sullivan tried Gilbert again in January 1889, wanting him to tackle a dramatic work on a big scale. To some extent *The Yeoman of the Guard* had been a step towards this. But Gilbert refused once more.

There were also problems with the company and it was breaking up. George Grossmith was planning to go back to his job as a piano entertainer, Barrington had already left the company, Temple and Ulmar wanted to leave and Bond wanted more money. Sullivan did not want to break up his partnership with Gilbert and actually saw the impending breakup of the company as being an ideal way to rekindle their partnership on a completely different footing.

Soon D'Oyly Carte would be brought into the argument between Gilbert and Sullivan. There had always been problems with either Gilbert or Sullivan accusing the other of interference, time wasting or ruining one another's work. With one of Sullivan's letters in his hand, D'Oyly Carte took a cab to Harrington Gardens to show it to Gilbert:

'They are Gilbert's pieces with music added by me. You can hardly wonder that twelve years of this has a little tired me and that unless a change in the construction of the piece and in the manner of rehearsing and producing it is made I should wish to give it up altogether. You had better bring the substance of this letter to Gilbert's notice. If he thinks all I say unreasonable there is an end of the matter. If he is disposed to meet my views in all these matters we can see about a new piece at once. I write to you because I hate quarrelling with old friends and I should certainly say something unfortunate if I wrote to Gilbert.'

Gilbert was already 10 days into the work on the first draft of *The Gondoliers*. He was clearly incensed by what he had read and wrote back to Sullivan:

'[The letter to Carte] teamed with unreasonable demands and utterly groundless accusations, the very least of which, if it had the smallest basis of truth, would suffice to disqualify me absolutely from collaboration with you. You say that our operas are Gilbert's pieces with music added by you, and that Carte can hardly wonder that twelve years of this has tired you. I say that when you deliberately assert that for twelve years you, uncomparably the greatest English musician of the age – a man whose genius is a proverb where the English tongue is spoken – a man who can deal 'en prince' with operatic managers, singers, music publishers and musical societies – when you, who hold this unparalleled position deliberately state that you have submitted silently and uncomplainingly for twelve years to be extinguished, ignored, set aside, rebuffed, and generally effaced by your librettist, you grievously reflect, not upon him, but upon yourself and the noble art of which you are so eminent a professor.'

The quarrel between the two men was settled on May 9, 1889. It took place with D'Oyly Carte acting as the peacemaker, as he wrote:

'I went to Paris to see Sullivan and came back with him and after much conversation and negotiations the position is now this. Sullivan is prepared to write with you at once another comic opera for the Savoy on the old lines, if you are willing also. His aspirations in another direction [the grand opera] being satisfied, he will be, and is, the more ready to write a piece of the character we have hitherto found so successful. I think too that he really wishes to keep up the old collaboration, as I do. At one time as you know I was desirous of transferring the whole thing to the new theatre, but as you objected I gave up the idea, and have today declined an offer of £5,000 a year for the Savoy. Sullivan says he is ready to start work energetically as soon as you give him the material.'

Sullivan set about writing *The Gondoliers* and the grand opera, *Ivanhoe*, at the same time, with the words written by Julian Sturgis. Gilbert was also deeply involved in building the Garrick Theatre and he leased it to his friend, John Hare. Part of the argument between Gilbert and Sullivan had clearly sunk in and *The Gondoliers* opened with around 18 minutes of uninterrupted music. It also has the longest vocal score of all of their operas. But it was no easy job; eight of the numbers had to be reset by

Sullivan before everyone was happy with them. Working on the comic opera and the grand opera at the same time exhausted Sullivan.

The Gondoliers

The Gondoliers was a satire on social snobbery and republicanism. Many believe that the opera itself is really about Gilbert and Sullivan. Both men ruled together, but apart, and this was the only way that they could both be fulfilled.

The Times reviewed *The Gondoliers* on Monday, December 9, 1889:

'*The Gondoliers; or, the King of Barataria*, the new opera by Mr. Gilbert and Sir Arthur Sullivan, was received on Saturday night with such hearty and unanimous approbation as to make it easy to augur that it will be long before the next of the series is required. If a position among the best of the joint authors' productions be ultimately accorded to the new work, as will probably be the case, it will be due less to any remarkable originality or interest in the plot than to the dialogue, which is in Mr. Gilbert's very best style, and the bright and sparkling music, some of which is quite irresistible in its melodious gaiety, while all is, as usual, spontaneous, refined, and thoroughly characteristic of the composer. In its combination of extreme complexity with almost complete absence of incident the story rivals that of *Il Trovatore*, which it resembles in one important point.

The facts appear to be as follows (we undertake their relation with extreme diffidence):– The infant son of the King of Barataria, after being contracted in marriage to the daughter of a Castilian hidalgo, is "changed at nurse" for the son of his foster-mother, who at the time when the action of the piece takes place (1750) has become the wife of "a highly respectable and old-established brigand, who carries on an extensive practice in the mountains around Cordova." The substituted child is next carried off by the Grand Inquisitor of Spain, in consequence of the addiction of the Baratarian Court to the tenets of Wesleyan Methodism, to Venice, and is there once more mixed up with the son of a gondolier; the boys grow up together and pass as brothers, themselves becoming gondoliers and marrying Venetian contadine. That there has been what may be called a double shuffle is, of course, concealed from the audience until the end. The arrival of Inez, the nurse, who alone can declare which is the true King, is imminent all through the two acts, into which, according to precedent, the opera is divided; as the Inquisitor declares early in the first act that he can find her at any moment, the audience can but hope that something may delay her coming, and the consequent fall of the curtain, until a sufficient number of songs and concerted pieces have been heard. This delay is, of course, effected; and a new set of complications is occasioned by the revelation that neither of the gondoliers is King, but that one of them is her son. As it is absolutely impossible to tell which of the reputed brothers is the Spaniard and which the Italian, the second instalment of what we quite understand Mr. Gilbert calling a "dull enigma" is left untouched, or perhaps kept back for future occasions.

On this not very promising framework the author has constructed a libretto which even he has rarely surpassed in whimsical absurdity. Mr. Gilbert is a privileged person, and none but the most captious of critics will resent his allowing the Spanish Inquisitor, a functionary who rejoices in the name of Don Alhambra del Bolero (Mr. W. H. Denny), to reside, to all appearances permanently, in the Ducal Palace at Venice, and there to receive the state visit of an impoverished nobleman, the Duke of Plaza-Toro (Mr. F. Wyatt), who arrives with his Duchess (Miss Brandram), their daughter Casilda (Miss Decima Moore), who will be recognized as Queen of Barataria as soon as the identity of that Monarch is established, and their suite, consisting exclusively of a private drummer (Mr. Brownlow). The entry of these august personages in their pompons but shabby clothes, and the quartet they sing, start the hilarity of the piece, which never flags from that moment.

The two gondoliers (Messrs. Courtice Pounds and Mr. Rutland Barrington (sic)) are meanwhile being married to their sweethearts (Miss Geraldine Ulmar and Miss Jessie Bond); the ceremony is just accomplished when they are informed by the Inquisitor that one of them is King of Barataria; as it is at present impossible to decide which it is, both sail off in a very picturesque xebecque for the island of Barataria, there (wherever it may be) to reign jointly "as one individual".Their song sung in alternate syllables, by the two as they stand in an absurd attitude suggestive of the Siamese twins, is one of the great "hits" of the opera.

In the second act they are found enthroned side by side, after the manner of the two Kings of Brentford in the Duke of Buckingham's immortal travesty, but surrounded by a Court modelled on Republican principles. All departments rank equally, and everybody is at the head of his "department". It may be readily imagined that so excellent an opportunity for the exhibition of the characteristic Gilbertian humour is not lost. The Kings are apparently the only hard worked people in the realm, as it appears from Mr. Barrington's deliciously funny catalogues of the duties of the position, which range from dressing the private valet ("It's a rather nervous duty; he's a touchy little man") to running on little errands for the Minister of State. The courtiers, it should be added, are the chorus of gondoliers of the first act, and on the arrival of all the contadine, including the brides, there is, of course, great merrymaking. Once more the noble Spanish family arrives upon the scene, this time in gorgeous array, to claim the hand of whichever of the two Kings may prove to be Casilda's husband and the rightful monarch. The change in their circumstances has been effected by sundry means not unheard of outside Spain. The Duke drives a capital trade by getting

"Small titles and orders
For Mayors and Recorders,"

by floating bubble companies, and allowing ready made tailors to use his name,

"Though Robinson Crusoe
Would jib at their wearing apparel."

The Duchess adds to the family income by presenting

"any lady
Whose conduct is shady,"

and launching "her in first-rate society", by vowing her

"complexion
Derives its perfection
From somebody's soap – which it doesn't,"

and the like. Among the companies floated by the Duke, one is nothing less than himself, as appears in the first act; the joke is not carried far, but it gives opportunity for Casilda to prove her relationship to Miss Minnie Symperson and other creations of Mr. Gilbert's fancy, by asking, "Am I to understand that the Queen of Barataria may be called upon at any time to witness her honoured sire in process of liquidation?" and receiving the answer from her mother, "The speculation is not exempt from that drawback. If your father should stop it will, of course, be necessary to wind him up."

The situation in which three wives appear to belong to two husbands is finally cleared up by the declaration of the nurse (Miss Bernard) that neither of the two is King, but that the crown belongs to none other than Luiz the drummer, or "suite" of the Duke, to whom Casilda has already given her young affections.

All the qualities by which the music of the former operas has obtained for the series a popularity almost without parallel in musical history are present in the last of the set, and the average level of interest and beauty is in this instance higher than usual. Perhaps for that reason no individual song stands out from the rest as prominently as did "Were I thy bride" and "I have a song to sing, O," in its predecessor, but it cannot be doubted that nothing since the Mikado has been so good as the new work.

There is an abundance of charming concerted pieces, one of which, it is scarcely too much to say, is the cleverest thing that the composer has accomplished. It is a quartet in the second act, in which the two Kings and their respective wives endeavour to solve the difficulties of their position. Musically it is an elaborate set of variations on a very pretty theme. The subject is first sung through in unison and is then reiterated, always by three of the voices, each singer in turn descanting on it in tones of distraction or objurgation, and returning in succession to the calm and sedate theme. It was with great difficulty that the singers escaped with only one encore.

A quartet sung by the same singers in the first act, "Then one of us will be a queen," is less interesting from a musical point of view, but is scarcely less hilarious. When an attempt was made by Sir

Arthur Sullivan to repeat only the latter portion of the number, shouts of "All of it" obliged him to accept an inevitable fate, and allow the whole to be sung again.

In the course of the Inquisitor's song, "There lived a King, as I've been told," three exceedingly funny musical allusions occur, which scarcely need to be pointed out, so quickly were they taken up by the audience. The ensemble at the entry of the grandees "from the sunny Spanish shore," is as lively in music as it is in words, and the interludes on the side drum are very mirth-provoking.

One of the happiest touches of Mr. Gilbert's own humour immediately succeeds this, when the Duke observes that he would

A private performance of The Gondoliers *for Queen Victoria, at Windsor Castle, performed in 1891.*

have paid his state visit to the ducal palace in Venice on horseback, "but, owing, I presume, to an unusually wet season, the streets are in such a condition that equestrian exercise is impracticable."

The quintet in the second act, which takes the form of a lesson in deportment, given to the two Kings by the ducal family is an extremely pretty gavotte, with the quartette already mentioned and a very brilliant cachucha (not to mention another quintette strongly recalling the well-known ensemble in Carmen), it constitutes one of the chief musical attractions of that act, which, apart from these three, is less interesting than the first.

To mention all the successful numbers would be to make an exhaustive catalogue of the music. The Duke's song with a very skilful drum obligato, the duet for his daughter and the "suite", the Inquisitor's song, the charming bridal chorus, are thoroughly effective and bright. The songs for the two brides are less remarkable, for they conform to various types that have become a little too well worn in previous operas of the series. Ample compensation is given, however, in that part of the finale in which they entreat their husbands to behave with exemplary propriety in their new sphere. The whole is most skilfully orchestrated as usual.

A special interest attached to the present production altogether apart from its own qualities, in consequence of Mr. Barrington's return to the Savoy Theatre and Mr. Grossmith's absence for the first time, since the series began, from the first performance of a new opera. The former artist was greeted with a burst of hearty applause, the purpose of which was quite unmistakable; he acted and sang with all his usual unction, and his dancing was as excellent as ever. Mr. Grossmith must accidentally have entered his own name on a certain "list" about which he used to sing in The Mikado, for although the company would unquestionably be stronger than it is, were he present, yet it cannot be said that any very terrible blank is caused by his absence, and no trace is to be found of a part such as he alone could create, and such as was a principal attraction is one and all of the former operas.

Mr. Denny as the Grand Inquisitor is quite first-rate, and his demeanour, as he remarks, concerning the nurse who is waiting in the torture chamber to be "interviewed," "There's no hurry – she's all right. She has all the illustrated papers," reaches a very high standard of comic acting. Mr. F. Wyatt, a new acquisition to the company, is a legitimate successor to Mr. Temple; his singing and acting are very good, and he has the excellent support of Miss Brandram, who has a part that suits her to perfection. Miss Decima Moore, another new-comer, has a delightfully fresh voice, which it is to be hoped will not be materially injured by the wear and tear involved in singing elaborate music night after night; she sings with very good taste and gives distinct promise of becoming a very acceptable actress; her appearance is extremely taking, and on the whole, a more successful début has not recently taken place, at least in comic opera.

Miss Ulmar uses her powerful voice with considerable taste, and has made decided improvement since her first appearance. Miss Bond is of course the life and soul of the scenes in which the married couples take part; her singing, acting, and dancing are, as usual, superlatively good. Mr. Courtice Pounds is thoroughly satisfactory, though he is rather overshadowed by the constant companionship of Mr. Barrington. Mr. Brownlow in the small part of the real King, who is first seen as the "suite" of the Duke, has a voice which might prove agreeable if it could be heard without a constant tremolo.

The two scenes are a marvel of stage adaptation, the first representing no less a space than the Piazetta at Venice, with the columns of the Ducal palace and the lagoons beyond. The second, a very pretty scene of Moorish character, does not commit itself to any rash statements concerning the position of Barataria on the map. It is needless to say that with Sir Arthur Sullivan directing affairs the performance went without a hitch of any kind, and that the reception of the work could not possibly have been more cordial.'

The Gondoliers **Cast and Synopsis**

The Duke of Plaza-Toro	Frank Wyatt
Luiz	Wallace Brownlow
Don Alhambra del Bolero	William Henry Denny
Marco Palmieri	Courtice Pounds

Giuseppi Palmieri	Rutland Barrington
Antonio	A Metcalf
Francesco	Charles Rose
Giorgio	George de Pledge
Annibale	James Wilbraham
The Duchess of Plaza-Toro	Rosina Brandram
Casilda	Decima Moore
Gianetta	Geraldine Ulmar
Tessa	Jessie Bond
Fiametta	Nellie Lawrence
Vittoria	Annie Cole
Giulia	Norah Phyllis
Inez	Annie Bernard

Act I

The act opens with girls making bouquets and singing about their love of Marco and Guiseppi. The brothers choose their brides using blind man's bluff and select Gianett and Tessa. Everyone then goes to the church for the weddings. Casilda was married as a child to a prince who is now the king of Barataria and she has arrived with her parents, the Duke and Duchess. They have come to Venice to ask the Grand Inquisitor, Don Alhambra as to the king's whereabouts. Secretly Casilda has fallen in love with Luiz. The Grand Inquisitor tells them that he was kidnapped and taken to Venice and is believed to be living with the Palmieris family. Unfortunately, the foster father was a keen drinker and could not tell the difference between his own son and the king. Only his foster mother, Inez, knows who is who. She is now summoned. Meanwhile, the weddings have taken place and the shock news is that one of the brothers is actually the king of Barataria. Until Inez can tell which one is the king they will both rule and they leave for Barataria.

Act II

Some three months have passed and the brothers have given all the gondoliers important court positions. The brothers' wives have not been allowed to join them but now they arrive and celebrations are planned for the reunion. Don Alhambra tells the brothers that one of them is already married to Casilda, so one of them is a bigamist. The Duke and

Duchess, along with Casilda, arrive. The confusion is resolved when Inez appears and tells everyone that she actually swapped her own son for the king when there was a threat of the child being kidnapped again. She brought the king up as her own son, so Luiz is in fact the king. Luiz becomes king and Casilda his queen, allowing the gondoliers to return to Venice with their wives.

The Gondoliers ran for 554 performances. It should be noted that Rutland Barrington had returned to the company, after a financially

MISS JESSIE BOND & MR. RUTLAND BARRINGTON.
"On the Road."

After the temporary break up of Gilbert and Sullivan's partnership, following The Gondoliers, *Jessie Bond and Rutland Barrington left D'Oyly Carte in 1891 and toured, performing songs and sketches. This is an illustration by Alfred Bryan.*

Mr. W. S. Gilbert: "Well, D'Oyly, and when do you think you will want me again?"

An Alfred Bryan cartoon, probably dated around 1891, which pokes fun at the temporary break up of Gilbert and Sullivan's partnership during the performances of Sullivan's grand opera, Ivanhoe.

disastrous period at St James's Theatre. The audience was extremely appreciative of the new opera and the critics praised it. However it was not so popular in the United States and lacked financial success there.

D'Oyly Carte's new theatre opened with *Ivanhoe* on January 31 1891, running for 155 performances. The Royal English Opera House did not last very long and it became the Palace Theatre Music Hall in 1892.

The Carpet Quarrel

Within nine months of the success of *The Gondoliers* Gilbert, Sullivan and D'Oyly Carte were at loggerheads. It was a flashback to some of the quarrels that the three had had over the division of profit after expenses. Gilbert had been in India and Sullivan had spent a considerable amount of time touring around Europe.

Gilbert wrote to Sullivan:

'I have had difficulty with Carte. I was appalled to learn from him the preliminary expenses of *The Gondoliers* amounted to the stupendous sum of £4,500! This seemed so utterly unaccountable that I asked to see the details and last night I received a resume of them. this includes such trifles as £75 for Miss Moore's second dress – £50 for her first dress – £100 for Miss Brandram's second dress (this costly garment has now, for some occult reason, been sent on tour); £450 for the wages of the carpenters during the time they were engaged on the scenery; £460 for the gondola, the sailing boat, the two columns and the two chairs and fountain for Act II; £112 for timber, £120 for ironmongery, £95 for canvas – and so forth. But the most surprising item was £500 for new carpets for the front of the house.'

A meeting between Gilbert and D'Oyly Carte went part of the way to solve the so-called carpet quarrel. He would accept that expenses related to the theatre itself would not be deducted from profits, but that it would mean that the rent for the Savoy Theatre would increase from £4,000 to £5,000. Gilbert expected Sullivan to back him up but he did not. In fact the carpet itself had not cost £500 but £140. D'Oyly Carte accepted that the costs of *The Gondoliers* were enormous, but put the blame on Gilbert, saying that he had given instructions to the costume designers and to other suppliers without any reference to himself. D'Oyly Carte was also firmly of the opinion that the wear and tear on the Savoy Theatre was down to the partnership and was a legitimate expense. D'Oyly Carte clearly thought that Gilbert and Sullivan were getting the best of the deal anyway and that where there were losses it was he that was bearing them and not the writing partnership:

'When you return all you do is to come to the Savoy Theatre and create disturbances. I should be very sorry to lose the pecuniary advantage of the productions of future operas of yours, but the earth does not contain the money that would pay me to put up with this sort of thing. To conclude, if you are dissatisfied with the accounts, every facility can be given you to check them. The question, if it can be called a question, as to what should be charged against profits seems to be a very simple one and I cannot conceive how it could be argued that the restoring of carpets worn out, upholstery, and painting, etc where necessary, should not come under the heading of repairs necessitated by wear and tear, just as much as the renewals of electric lamps as they wear out. I believe it is custom for all lessees of theatres to pay out such expenses. The Savoy is put out at less than lease price and out of that reduced price I could and should certainly not undertake to pay such expenses, as I have never agreed to. The argument speaks for itself.'

Sullivan's lack of support was now threatening an irretrievable break between the two men. Gilbert wrote to Sullivan on May 5, 1890:

'The time for putting an end to our partnership has at last arrived. I am writing a letter to Carte giving him notice that he is not to produce or perform any of my libretti after Christmas 1890. In point of fact, after the withdrawal of *The Gondoliers*, our united work will be heard in public no more.'

Despite attempts to cool the situation down, Gilbert had already put the matter into the hands of his solicitors. Carte followed suit. Gilbert issued a writ and Sullivan tried to get the two men to at least talk. Helen Carte met with Gilbert on September 15 and told him that her husband, Richard, would be willing to make a settlement. Gilbert appears to have been adamant about his point of view and wanted to open all of the accounts back to the start of the partnership and re-examine them. This was turning into an unholy mess.

Towards the end of September Sullivan wrote to Gilbert, almost begging him to bring the argument to an end:

'I am physically and mentally ill over this wretched business. I have not yet got over the shock of seeing our names coupled not in brilliant collaboration over a work destined for worldwide celebration, but in hostile antagonism over a few miserable pounds.'

There was a crumb of comfort for Sullivan and D'Oyly Carte with the opening of *Ivanhoe* in January 1891. But Gilbert refused to attend.

Meanwhile, Gilbert, using Alfred Cellier to write the music, put on *The Mountebanks* at the Lyric Theatre. It opened on January 4, 1892 and had a reasonable run of 229 performances. D'Oyly Carte had to look for another pairing to produce a comic opera for the Savoy after *The Gondoliers* ended its run. It was *The Nautch Girl* by George Dance and Edward Solomon and it ran for 200 performances.

Gilbert and Sullivan were, to a large extent, reconciled and Gilbert visited Sullivan in December 1892, just before Sullivan was due to travel abroad. Gilbert mentioned an idea about an opera on a south sea island. They met again in April 1893 on the Riviera and Gilbert presented Sullivan with his plot for *Utopia Limited*.

Chapter 6

The Last Collaborations

Utopia Limited

Opera number 13, *Utopia Limited*, opened on October 7, 1893. The casting was somewhat different than before, as it required accomplished singers and an ability to play a comedy role. Some of the old members of the company, such as George Grossmith and Jessie Bond, were there for the first night. The music for the opera had been begun by Sullivan in the June and he finished Act I in a month; Gilbert was delighted with the finale. The pair quarrelled over Act II and relations became strained once more. Gilbert was particularly bad tempered because of his gout.

It was to become the most expensive of all of the Savoy operas, costing a massive £7,200 to put on. It also had the longest first act and before cuts were made the first act ran for an hour and three-quarters. Once again

Gilbert reading the libretto of Utopia Limited *on the first day of rehearsal at the Savoy Theatre.*

Gilbert had plundered his back catalogue and had used one of his early plays, *The Happy Land* (1873) as background. It was a satire of party politics, local government and law. It had a relatively straightforward plot.

The Times reviewed the opera on October 9, 1893:

'The resumption of the famous association of Sir Arthur Sullivan with Mr. Gilbert, an association which was so fruitful of mirth in the past, gave a very special interest to the first night of the new opera, *Utopia (Limited)*, on Saturday night. No doubt Mr. Carte would have found it convenient to enlarge his theatre to three times its size, for it is said on good authority that the demand for seats at the production was greater than on any former occasion. The general rejoicing over the renewal of joint work by the author and composer, who have worked so long and successfully together, was so deeply felt that the success of the new piece would have been assured had either words or music, or both, been below the level of the best of the series. Happily, however, the occasion seems to have put each of the two upon his mettle, and the result is that the latest is also one of the best of the set. Since *The Mikado*, indeed, it is hard to remember any work of the same hands that is worthy to stand beside the new production for pointed dialogue and easily-assimilated music.

As usual, the action occupies two extremely long acts, but it cannot be said that there is a single dull moment from beginning to end, and this in spite of the almost complete absence of anything in the shape of plot, or even of thorough development of the central idea of the piece, which is as whimsical, though by no means as original, as ever. The introduction of English manners and customs into remote or imaginary countries has furnished forth many a piece of satire, whether on the stage or off, and at this very moment an entertainment, still enjoying a successful run, has precisely the same motive as the new Savoy opera, although it need hardly be said that the advantages in respect of wit, refinement, and charm of every kind are on the side of the newer production.

The King of Utopia has sent his eldest daughter to be educated at Girton, for he and his people have the most exalted ideas concerning all things English, ideas which are illustrated in the existence of a scurrilous society paper, the Palace Peeper, devoted to sham revelations of the iniquities of the Court, all of which are written by the King himself. In order to complete the Anglicizing of the land, the Princess brings with her, not only an escort of Life Guards, but six chosen specimens of British civilization, "Flowers of Progress", consisting of an officer from each service, a Lord Chamberlain, a Judge, a County Councillor, and a company promoter, the last of whom takes immediate steps to run the kingdom as a limited liability concern. The audience, accustomed to the process that has become classical in such pieces, expects the second act to exhibit all manner of weak points in the new order of things, and to land the persons of the drama in inextricable confusion owing to the effort to carry the new doctrines to a logical close.

Here Mr. Gilbert is one too many for his public, for, instead of this, all goes well, and the only objection to the innovation is made on the score that war, crime, and disease have completely disappeared. The two Judges of the Utopian Supreme Court have been making a good thing out of various schemes which are now stultified, and they stir up the people of Utopia to rebellion against the English influence, by "making an affidavit that what they supposed to be happiness was really unspeakable misery", and peace is only restored when the Princess hits upon the happy idea of introducing the great principle of "government by party", by means of which the disastrous prosperity of the nation will be put an end to. Mr. Gilbert has not often appeared as the preacher of a political creed, but here he has directed all his satire against the enemies of progress, and in another direction shows a marked approval of a modern type of young ladyhood, describing as the "typical English girl" a creature "of magnificent comeliness … of 11 stone two, and five feet ten in her dancing shoe." Fortunately no loud-voiced hoyden is presented as the fulfilment of the ideal, but the figure of the Princess Zara is one of great charm and distinction, even apart from the decidedly successful impersonation given by Miss Nancy M'Intosh, (sic) a débutante who won golden opinions on Saturday.

As a rule, it is only too easy to refer to the specially good points of such productions as this, whether in words or music; here it is quite impossible to give even a bare catalogue of the amusing things in the opera, or of the numbers in the score that will catch the public ear. The most hilarious concerted pieces, "patter songs", topical duets of the approved pattern, succeed one another with bewildering speed, and the dialogue that separates them is so uniformly funny that it scarcely performs its original functions of allowing breathing space between the musical portions.

The overture, it is true, is meagre in extent and poor in quality, consisting of little more than a trivial tune employed afterwards to accompany the ceremonial at the drawing-room held by Princess Zara on the English model (with certain improvements – such as the choice of the evening rather than the afternoon, and the "cheap and effective inspiration" of "a cup of tea and a plate of mixed biscuits"). The King's song, with its pretty introductory chorus for female voices, and its effective accompaniment, as of "tyrant thunder", on the big drum, serves to introduce Mr. Barrington in a more or less familiar way, and the scene which immediately follows is one of the best in the piece.

Rutland Barrington as King Paramount in Utopia Limited.

The two younger Princesses, who are twins, have been brought up as model English young ladies by a governess, Lady Sophy who "unconsciously exercises a weird and supernatural fascination over all Crowned Heads." The perfect deportment of her charges is daily exhibited to the populace, and she delivers a lecture on "the course of maiden courtship", illustrated in dumb show by the twins, whose demure behaviour suggests that they are less innocent than they look. The waltz tune to which the lecture is set is scarcely among the best of the composer's inventions in this kind, but the whole scene is admirable and excellently played.

A fairly characteristic song and trio on the subject of life's grim jests, between the King and the two Judges, is exceedingly funny; and the courtship scene between the monarch and the governess is most diverting and charmingly set. The "dance of repudiation" is one of several jokes concerning the fatuity of descriptive dancing. The song with the choral refrain "The First Life Guards", which follows the entry of the Princess and her escort, is very taking and one of the sure successes of the piece, although the solo soprano music is neither very prominent nor very grateful.

The introduction of the six representatives of progress brings about a delightful quotation from *H.M.S. Pinafore*, which was received on Saturday with shouts of applause.

The second act opens with a tenor solo for the Princess's lover, Captain Fitzbattleaxe, illustrating most amusingly the impossibility of maintaining perfect vocalization in the expression of a veritable emotion. Here, and elsewhere, Mr. Kenningham was excellent, and his thoroughly finished singing enabled him to give point to the musical phrases in which he is supposed to break down. One very old and respectable pantomime device which occurs at the end of each verse, where a note missed by the singer is supplied, a semitone too high, by the clarinet, might well be reconsidered, as it does not do much to enhance the point of the joke.

The Cabinet Council, which is suddenly transformed into a Christy Minstrel performance, is sure to receive the honour of a double encore, conferred upon it on Saturday; and the drawing-room: scene, preceded by the King's command, "Let the revels commence," is likely to prove a popular spectacle, though the ladies' dresses are not particularly successful from a decorative point of view. One of many momentary allusions to English national tunes occurs at its close; and finally a hymn-like chorus, unaccompanied, is sung by all the characters.

The capital trio of the two Judges and the official called the "Public Exploder" leads to a series of love scenes, at the climax of which the King and Lady Sophy are discovered by the younger couples, and all take part in a sufficiently bright tarantella. The entry of the discontented population and their chorus, "Down with the Flowers of Progress" is a little too closely modelled upon "Stone him to death" in St. Paul, and the finale of the whole is disappointingly slight; still, there is so much that is in the best vein of both author and composer that this may well be pardoned.

Mr. Rutland Barrington, as the King, sings and acts in his usual style and with perfect success, though it could be wished that he danced a little more. Messrs. Denny and Le Hay are admirably funny as the two Judges, and their dresses in the first act, like those of all the Utopians, are pleasantly fantastic. Mr. Scott Fishe, as the company promoter, has one or two good songs to sing, and sings them well; and Mr. W. Passmore is duly energetic as Tarara, the Public Exploder.

Miss Nancy M'Intosh sings and acts in a way that promises excellently for her future career, if she elects to forsake the work of a concert singer, in which she has already made a most successful start. She is a most refined representative of the Princess, and her delivery of her spoken lines, particularly of a speech in which she quotes from "An expurgated Juvenal", is extremely good. Nervousness impaired her vocal powers on Saturday, so that her charming voice made less than its usual effect; but this will no doubt be soon overcome, and the assumption will then reach a very high point of excellence. Miss Rosina Brandram, as Lady Sophy, adds a new impersonation to the long series of her successful performances in the same kind. She won much applause, not only for her lecture, but for the sentimental song which is almost a foregone conclusion in her parts. Misses Emmie Owen and Florence Perry are suitably demure and sly as the twin Princesses. An irritating habit of pronouncing the word "England" in the

THE SAVOY.

THE ENTR'ACTE, *loq.* :—" Glad to see you together, gentlemen. You'll find this more profitable than pulling different ways."

Richard D'Oyly Carte, W S Gilbert and Arthur Sullivan together for Utopia Limited *after a long quarrel. Dated 1893 – drawing by Alfred Bryan.*

German way prevailed in the earlier scenes, but was gradually given up; it may be expected to disappear as the run of the piece goes on.

The performance, directed by the composer, was in all respects excellent, and the collaborators were most enthusiastically cheered at the close of the performance.'

Utopia Limited ran for 245 performances and had the subtitle *Flowers of Progress*. Again it was a two-act comic opera.

Utopia Limited Cast and Synopsis

King Paramount the First	Rutland Barrington
Scaphio	William Henry Denny

Phantis	John le Hay
Tartara	Walter Parsmore
Calynx	Bowden Haswell
Princess Zara	Nancy McIntosh
Princess Nekeya	Emmie Owen
Princess Kalyba	Florence Perry
Lady Sophy	Rosina Brandram
Salata	Edith Johnson
Melene	May Bell
Phylla	Florence Easton
Lord Dramaleigh	Scott Russell
Captain Fitzbattleaxe	Charles Kenningham
Captain Sir Edward Corcoran	Lawrence Gridley
Mr Goldbury	Scott Fishe
Sir Bailey Barre	Enes Blackmore
Mr Blushington	Herbert Ralland

Act I

The act opens with the women of Utopia in the Royal Gardens. They are told by Calynx that Zara is coming home from England and wants to anglicise Utopia. A banned newsletter, *The Palace Peeper*, has contained news of the king's supposed immorality and the Public Exploder Tarara is angry because he has not been ordered to kill the king. Scaphio and Phantis are the real power in Utopia. Phantis loves Zara and Scaphio promises to help him win her heart. The real writer of *The Palace Peeper* is King Paramount himself, forced to write it by Scaphio and Phantis. The king does not wish Zara to see the newsletter, nor for that matter Lady Sophy, whom he loves. Sophy appears and she has a copy of the newsletter but because the king refuses to try to find out who wrote the articles she rebuffs his advances. Zara arrives accompanied by the lifeguards and Fitzbattleaxe. Scaphio falls for her and both he and Phantis tell her of their love for her. Fitzbattleaxe also loves Zara and he suggests that he will look after her whilst Scaphio and Phantis fight a duel to the death for her hand. Zara sees the newsletter and confronts the king. He breaks down, telling her the truth. Zara then tells the king that she has brought with her six Flowers of Progress. They will help change Utopia and oust Scaphio and Phantis. The king wants to learn more and he and the court accept the plans, which include Utopia being a limited monarchy.

Act II

The first cabinet meeting is held. Scaphio and Phantis threaten the king but he will not listen to them and they go to Tarara, claiming that the king is committing treason. The Flowers of Progress try to explain to the princesses that English girls are not necessarily perfect. Sophy will not marry anyone but a perfect monarch and she has read the articles, believing the king to be fatally flawed. The king tells her the truth and she is delighted. Their embrace is witnessed by all, but Scaphio and Phantis have organised a rebellion because Utopia is now too perfect. Zara then realises what the problem is; there is no party politics. If she introduces party politics then one party can undo what the other has done. The king is happy to accept this and Scaphio and Phantis are arrested.

The Savoy actually lost money on the production and not all of the critics were supportive of the new opera; some recognised that it was a travesty of the work that they had done in the past. Gilbert and Sullivan had scrapped the finale and a new one was introduced after just four days.

Gilbert toyed with the idea of a new opera with Sullivan in January 1894, but instead he produced *His Excellency*, with music by F Osmond Carr for the Lyric Theatre. *Utopia Limited* came off in the summer of 1894 and there was nothing to replace it. Sullivan had been in Berlin conducting *Ivanhoe* and looking over a German production of *The Gondoliers*. He composed music for a play at the Lyceum, *King Arthur*, and all that could be done was to bring back *The Mikado* to the Savoy.

In October 1895 Jessie Bond asked Gilbert if she could have a new song for *The Mikado* revival. He replied:

'Even if we could find a place for it (very difficult), there is Sullivan to be reckoned with and I doubt very much if he would care to put aside the new piece upon which he is working night and day, in order to write a song for Mikado. He is like me in one respect (only in one) – when he is in full swing of his work, as he is now, he won't stand interruption.'

The new piece of work that Sullivan was now working on was the fourteenth and last Gilbert and Sullivan piece, *The Grand Duke*.

The Grand Duke

The Mikado revival ran for 127 performances and in fact this would be longer than *The Grand Duke*. *The Mikado* would return with a run of 226 performances after *The Grand Duke* had closed.

In August 1895 Gilbert had read the plot to Sullivan and he had written back:

'I have studied the sketch plot very carefully and like it even more than I did when I heard it first on Thursday. It comes out as clear and bright as possible and I shall be very pleased to set it, and am prepared to begin (as soon as you have anything ready for me) and have written to Carte to tell him so.'

Helen Carte had been the driving force behind getting Gilbert and Sullivan to collaborate for one last opera. Her husband was unwell; Sullivan was suffering from his kidney problems and Gilbert from another bout of gout. As it was *The Grand Duke* collapsed after 123 performances. The rehearsals had commenced in January 1896. There would be no George Grossmith, Jessie Bond or Richard Temple. By any stretch of the imagination, the plot to *The Grand Duke* was somewhat tired.

The plot told the story of members of a theatrical troupe who were actually acting out the roles that they were supposed to perform. Central to the story was a duel and cutting a pack of cards. It was really about social roles obscuring someone's real identity.

The Times reviewed *The Grand Duke* on March 9, 1896:

'The welcome accorded to a new Gilbert-and-Sullivan opera increases, perhaps not unnaturally, with each member of the famous series, and its warmth is all the greater on account of the regrettable intermissions in the partnership. But the former works themselves are, as usual, the severest critics of the newer; and, in the case of the opera produced on Saturday night, the recent revival of the best of the whole set inevitably provokes awkward comparisons. *The Grand Duke* is not by any means another Mikado, and, though it is far from being the least attractive of the series, signs are not wanting that the rich vein which the collaborators and their various followers have worked for so many years is at last dangerously near

Ilka von Palmay, who played Julia Jellicoe in The Grand Duke.

exhaustion. This time the libretto is very conspicuously inferior to the music. There are still a number of excellent songs, but the dialogue seems to have lost much of its crispness, the turning-point of what plot there is requires considerable intellectual application before it can be thoroughly grasped, and some of the jests are beaten out terribly thin. There is doubtless much still to be made out of the time-honoured jokes on the parsimonious disposition of the smaller German Courts; but to occupy the greater half of an exceedingly long act with virtually nothing else is surely a mistake on Mr. Gilbert's part. The less intricate conditions of the "statutory duel" which provides the sub-title for the piece are that the combatants settle their differences by means of drawing cards; the holder of the lower card forthwith becomes civilly dead, and the survivor takes over his responsibilities, including his poor relations, and generally steps into his shoes. After two such encounters, the leading actor in the theatrical company of Speisesaal succeeds to the position, first of his own manager, and shortly afterwards to that of the Grand Duke, who, hearing of a conspiracy to blow him up, is only too ready to arrange that, while he draws a king, the comedian shall draw an ace and enter into his dignities. As the actor is on the eve of marriage with the soubrette of the troupe, and as a rule has been passed that stations about the Court shall be distributed to the company according to professional position, the leading lady, with feigned reluctance, feels bound to undertake the part of the Grand Duchess; the elderly fiancée of the real Grand Duke insists on being transferred to the new ruler, and finally the Princess of Monte Carlo, to whom the Duke was betrothed in infancy, turns up unexpectedly and establishes her prior rights. The resuscitation of the manager and the Grand Duke is contrived by the discovery of a rule that the ace shall rank as lowest card of the pack, and of course the various ladies, some of whom appear to have been actually married to the actor, find suitable partners before the fall of the curtain.

Though there are next to no topical allusions, the dialogue has a considerable number of whimsical ideas, and when these have been brought nearer to each other by the compression of much that makes the first act and the latter part of the second seem a little tedious, their effect will, no doubt, be increased. "Drains that date back to the reign of Charlemagne" is a phrase that deserves to pass into the language; the ceremonial observed by the seven chamberlains, and their costumes, carefully graduated in the matter of ornament according to their official rank; the adoption of Greek costume by the actor-duke and his Court, he himself appearing in a splendid Louis XIV wig; and the "job lot" of noblemen, hired from a Jew costumier by the Prince of Monte Carlo – these are among the best things in the piece.

It is a good many years since the composer has given us anything so fine as the opening chorus of the second act, with a sham-Greek refrain, a melody so spontaneous, dignified, and original that it seems hardly suited to its surroundings, or to the taste of most of the audience. From this point, up to and including the tuneful song in which the herald introduces the Prince of Monte Carlo, is, musically speaking, the best part of the work; the actor-duke's exceedingly funny song about the manners and customs of ancient Greece, the clever duet in which the "leading lady" gives her "notion of a first-rate part", her scene "So ends my dream",written in evident imitation and derision of the conventional operatic aria of the last generation, and the elderly baroness's drinking song, which sets out with a reminiscence of the Irish tune "Kate Kearney", are all certain to be popular. The first act contains a number of pretty choruses, some concerted vocal numbers as effective as usual, and a capital march of the chamberlains, all neatly finished and in strict conformity with the pattern established for such things a good many years ago. That form of instrumental humour, in which Sir Arthur Sullivan has delighted ever since the famous "bassoon joke" in *The Sorcerer*, finds excellent opportunity in a song in which the grand duke describes his ailments, to the accompaniment of some orchestral symptoms so realistic as to be almost painful. After the entry of the Monte Carlo family in the second act the music is of slighter importance, and the prince's song, in the course of which a roulette table is produced, males remarkably little effect. The overture consists of a string of tunes that are likely to be most popular.

The "topsy-turvy" element that is looked for in Mr. Gilbert's work is provided by the curious expedient of giving the part of the leading lady of the theatrical company, an English comedian, to a foreign singer, whose broken English is to be taken as representing the broken German of the English performer in a German company. The thing is a little hard to realize, but as the pretty broken English of the singer was greeted with roars of laughter the curious device must be considered successful. The distinguished Hungarian soubrette Mme. Ilka von Palmay, who made her first appearance in London last summer with the Saxe-Coburg Company, has considerably improved and toned down her method, or possibly she is fortunately hampered by her incomplete command of English. Her voice, though far from pleasing, is used with much art, and her delivery of the song in the second act, with its cantabile beginning and brilliant close, fully deserved the encore it received on Saturday. Her resources were fully equal to the scene in which she gives a burlesque specimen of tragic acting, and throughout the second act at least she was entirely successful. Miss Florence Perry, who must be warned against a growing tendency both to force her small voice and to overact, wins much approval in the part of Lisa; Miss Emmie

Owen makes the most of the small part of the princess; and Miss Rosina Brandram is as artistic as ever in the part of the baroness, adding yet another to her series of careful portraits of elderly and amorous ladies. Mr. Rutland Barrington, on whom, as now usual, falls the chief burden of the piece, is intensely funny as Ludwig, more especially in the absurd costume of the second act, of which the most is made. Mr. Charles Kenningham sings the part of the manager with much care, but spoils it by exaggeration of gesture. Mr. Walter Passmore, in the character of the stingy and dyspeptic grand duke, comes nearer to Mr. Grossmith's level than he has done yet, and his delivery of the songs is in some respects very good. The capital song in which he is obliged to keep back a sneeze until his handkerchief is pompously handed from the "Acting-Temporary-Sub-Deputy-Assistant Vice-Chamberlain" to his superior, and so with much state from one of the seven officials to another, was received with much enthusiasm. Mr. Scott Fishe is an excellent Prince of Monte Carlo; but the effect of his roulette song is thrown into the shade by the herald's song with chorus, one of the most taking things in the opera, in which Mr. J. Hewson was deservedly encored. Mr. Scott Russell was successful as a notary with the engaging name of Dr. Tannhäuser, and the quintet in which he took part in the first act was encored. The same compliment was bestowed on Mr. Barrington's two songs, the first of which relates the awkward effects of carrying out too faithfully the rule of the secret society which orders the consumption of a sausage-roll as the sign of confederacy; on Lisa's pretty song, in which she commends the faithless Ludwig to her rival's care; on the soprano scene already mentioned; and on the herald's song. The chorus and orchestra are excellent as usual. On Saturday night the opera was conducted by the composer, and went without a hitch of any kind; and the famous Savoy triumvirate were called and warmly applauded at the end. The scenery, dresses, and mounting are as usual irreproachable, and the street perspective in the first scene is one of the most successful things of the kind ever seen on the stage.'

The subtitle of the opera was *The Statutory Duel*, billed as an original comic opera in two acts.

The Grand Duke Cast and Synopsis

Grand Duke Rudolph	Walter Passmore
Ernest Dummkopf	Charles Kenningham
Ludwig	Rutland Barrington
Dr Tannhäuser	Scott Russell
The Prince of Monte Carlo	Scott Fishe
Viscount Mentone	E Carleton
Ben Hasbaz	Charles Herbert Workman
Herald	Jones Hewson
Princess of Monte Carlo	Emmie Owen
Baroness von Krakenfeldt	Rosina Brandram
Julia Jellicoe	Ilka von Palmay
Lisa	Florence Perry
Olga	Mildred Baker
Gretchen	Ruth Vincent
Bertha	Jessie Rose
Elsa	Ethel Wilson
Martha	Beatrice Perry

Act I

A theatrical company, managed by Dummkopf, in the Grand Duchy of Pfennig-Halbpfennig, is celebrating the forthcoming marriage of Ludwig and Lisa. However, members of the company are involved in a plot to overthrow the Grand Duke and replace him with Ernest. Ernest has promised to find jobs for the theatrical troupe as members of his court. Behind this is the fact that the leading lady, Julia, will be compelled to marry Ernest. The plot is uncovered when Ludwig mistakenly tells the Grand Duke about the conspiracy. Dr Tannhäuser suggests that Ludwig and Ernest should duel, cutting a pack of cards. The winner will take the loser's responsibility and the loser will be considered dead. The winner will then see the Grand Duke, tell him that a conspiracy has been uncovered and that the leader of the conspiracy is dead. That would mean that the theatrical company would not be implicated. The loser could then reappear when a pardon has been granted. Ludwig wins and goes to see the Grand Duke but he is having his own problems; he was betrothed to the Princess of Monte Carlo as a child and he explains to his fiancé, Baroness von Krakenfeldt, that the betrothal will be rendered invalid by the following morning because the princess's father is too poor to make the journey to the Grand Duchy. The Grand Duke is told about the conspiracy by his detective and then Ludwig arrives. Ludwig suggests a duel so that the Grand Duke loses and gives up his title. The conspirators can then depose Ludwig and Rudolph could take back his throne. Ludwig wins the card duel and then the theatrical group discover what has been going on. Julia claims the role of Duchess, leaving Lisa broken hearted.

Act II

The baroness aims to claim Ludwig as her husband, leaving Julia deserted when Ludwig and the baroness decide to marry. The Prince of Monte Carlo arrives; he is no longer penniless as he has just invented the roulette wheel and is rich. He has appeared with the princess to claim the Grand Duke. The situation is solved when the notary explains that on each occasion Ludwig drew an ace and that in a statutory duel an ace is the lowest card, so Ludwig had in fact lost both duels. Rudolph, Ludwig and Ernest can now return to their former positions. The notary officiates over the marriage of Rudolph to the Princess of Monte Carlo, Ludwig to Lisa and Ernest to Julia.

The Grand Duke was very similar to Gilbert and Sullivan's *Thespis*, with the scene having been shifted from Mount Olympus to a Grand Duchy.

After *The Grand Duke* a new agreement was entered into between Gilbert and Sullivan and D'Oyly Carte. This allowed D'Oyly Carte to produce revivals of the operas at the Savoy. As we have already seen, *The Mikado* was revived after *The Grand Duke* collapsed. This was followed by *The Yeoman of the Guard*, then *The Gondoliers*, *The Sorcerer*, along with *Trial by Jury*, *HMS Pinafore*, *The Pirates of Penzance* and *Patience*.

As far as Gilbert and Sullivan were concerned this was to end their period of collaboration. By late 1898 Sullivan was seriously ill, but he was already planning to work on a new comic opera called *Hassan*, along with Basil Hood. It was completed in November 1899, under the title *The Rose of Persia*. It was very successful, running for 213 performances and many of the cast members were familiar Gilbert and Sullivan performers. In June 1900 Basil Hood sent Sullivan the outline for a new Irish-based opera, *The Emerald Isle*. Sullivan completed the *Te Deum* in July; this was his last piece of finished work, but it incorporated the tune *Onward Christian Soldiers* in the last chorus.

Sullivan returned to London in mid-September, with his health deteriorating. Neither Gilbert nor Sullivan had spoken to one another since September 22, 1898, at the revival of *The Sorcerer* and *Trial by Jury*. It had been planned for Sullivan to appear on stage for the revival of *Patience* in November 1900, but he was simply too ill. Gilbert and D'Oyly Carte appeared, both tottering on walking sticks.

Sullivan, at the age of 58, died after a heart attack on November 22. Gilbert was in Egypt, but he wrote to Sullivan's nephew, Herbert:

'I did not hear of your uncle's terribly sudden death until three days since, or I should have written to express my personal sorrow, and my sympathy with you in the great loss you have sustained. It is a satisfaction to me to feel that I was impelled, shortly before his death, to write to him to propose to shake hands over our recent differences, and an even greater satisfaction to learn through you that my offer of reconciliation was cordially accepted. I wish I had been in England that I might have had an opportunity of joining the mourners at his funeral.'

The missing pieces of work for *The Emerald Isle* were completed by Edward German and it opened at the Savoy in April 1901, running for 200 performances.

The next of the three partners to die was Richard D'Oyly Carte. He passed away on April 3, 1901, at the age of 56. By now things were changing and the Opera Comique had been demolished. Helen D'Oyly Carte took over the running of the Savoy Theatre, letting it out between 1902 and 1906, but then returning in the December.

Gilbert continued to supervise stage directions of revivals. He received £5,000 for performance rights for five years and a £200 rehearsal fee for each opera. Gilbert was now much more of a gentleman landowner and had settled into his house and grounds, Grim's Dyke, a mock Tudor mansion on Harrow Weald. He continued to work; even before Sullivan's death he had produced a number of works in collaboration with other composers. By 1910 Gilbert had sold performing rights to Helen D'Oyly Carte for a second term, but her management of the Savoy was coming to an end. She had, by now, remarried, but she died in 1913.

Gilbert's last literary work was a rewrite of *The Mikado*. This was in story form, but it did not come into print until ten years after his death.

Gilbert's home, Grim's Dyke, showing a garden party with innumerable actors and actresses, judges, bishops and statesmen.

His last play, *The Hooligan*, was performed at the Coliseum in February 1911. It involved the last hours of a condemned man.

The circumstances of Gilbert's death could not have been foreseen. It was May 29, 1911 and he had been in London during the morning, had lunched and then in the afternoon had arranged to teach two women to swim in the Grim's Dyke lake. One of the women got into problems in the water and Gilbert swam out to help her. He had a heart attack and drowned at the age of 74.

Sullivan had had a burial in St Paul's Cathedral, almost like a state funeral, by order of Queen Victoria. He was buried in the crypt despite his intention to be buried alongside his family members in Brompton cemetery. Gilbert was cremated at Golders Green and his remains buried at Great Stanmore churchyard. A memorial designed by Sir George Frampton was unveiled near the Embankment underground station in 1911. The inscription reads 'His foe was folly and his weapon wit'. His wife, Kitten, died in 1936.

One of the last comments that Gilbert ever made about Sullivan was full of generous praise:

'I remember all he has done for me in allowing his genius to shed some lustre upon my humble name. It is a source of gratification to me to reflect that the rift that parted us for a time was completely bridged over, and that, at the time of Sir Arthur Sullivan's lamented death, the most cordial relations existed between us.'

Chapter 7

The Great Performers

It would be impossible to detail the 3,000 or so performers that have appeared in Gilbert and Sullivan operas in D'Oyly Carte productions. We have therefore selected some of the mainstays of the company and those that appeared in multiple productions of the 14 operas throughout the years from 1875.

Barnett, Alice (d.1901)

She was a trained concert singer and joined the touring company as Little Buttercup for *HMS Pinafore* in 1879. She was given the role of Ruth in *The Pirates of Penzance* for the New York opening in December 1879. She returned to London in 1880. Gilbert thought she was ideal to play Lady Jane in *Patience* and the Queen of the Fairies in *Iolanthe*, possibly due to the fact that she was both tall and large. She suffered from ill-health, probably rheumatism, even at a relatively early age. When she returned to the company she found it difficult to displace Rosina Brandram, who had taken many of her potential roles. She therefore toured rather than appear in the main productions. She continued to perform in a number of other operas and spent three years in Australia playing Gilbert and Sullivan roles between 1885 and 1888. She returned to London in 1889 and toured Britain with a number of other opera companies. She appeared as Dame Cortlandt in Gilbert and Carr's *His Excellency* at the Lyric in October 1894 and later she toured America with the same production. She starred in *The Telephone Girl* in an English tour in May 1896 but was in another production in America in later 1896. She was back with *The Telephone Girl* in England in May 1897. She made her last appearance on a London stage in March 1900 and died of bronchial pneumonia following an operation on April 14 1901.

Barrington, Rutland (d.1919)

He created the role of Dr Daly in The Sorcerer in 1877 and went on to star in *Trial by Jury*, *HMS Pinafore*, *The Pirates of Penzance*, *Patience*, *Iolanthe* and *Princess Ida*. His most famous role was Pooh-Bah in *The Mikado* in 1885. He missed *The Yeoman of the Guard* but returned for *The Gondoliers*, leaving the company when *Utopia* closed in June 1894. He starred in several revivals and continued to perform until 1918. He was buried as a pauper in an unmarked grave at Morden cemetery until a granite marker was raised in 1997.

Billington, Fred (d.1917)

He was born in Lockwood, Huddersfield in 1854 and joined the touring company in Shoreditch in 1879 for *HMS Pinafore*. He also starred as the Sergeant of Police in the copyright performance of *The Pirates of Penzance* in Paignton in December 1879, before touring with *The*

A drawing of Fred Billington in his role as Pooh-Bah in The Mikado, *by C W Allers, dated 1888.*

Sorcerer and *HMS Pinafore* in 1880 and in the following year with *The Pirates of Penzance* and *HMS Pinafore*. By 1884 he was in the first provincial production of *Princess Ida*, going on to perform in *Trial by Jury* and *The Mikado*; the latter in the United States. He joined the continental touring company in May 1886, performing in Liverpool, Manchester and then Germany and Austria. In 1887 he rehearsed *Ruddigore* and gave two performances as Sir Despard Murgatroyd at the Savoy before making for New York, where he played the role until April 1887. He then toured in the same role in England and in the August he took Barrington's part at the Savoy. In September 1887 he was touring with *Patience* and *The Mikado* and *The Pirates of Penzance*. From 1888 to 1889 he toured with *HMS Pinafore*, *The Pirates of Penzance*, *Patience*, *The Mikado* and *The Yeoman of the Guard*. He was transferred to the United States to play Don Alhambra at the Palmer's Theatre in New York in February 1890 then he starred in the British tour of *The Gondoliers*, *The Mikado* and *The Yeoman of the Guard*. Billington worked tirelessly from 1890 to his death in 1917, playing a variety of roles in a number of Gilbert and Sullivan productions. He took the place of Rutland Barrington as Pooh-Bah in the revival of *The Mikado* at the Savoy between July and November 1896. He left the Savoy in April 1897 due to illness and returned to work with Company C for the rest of his career. Until the end he retained the parts of Sergeant of Police, Pooh-Bah, Shadbolt and Don Alhambra. On November 2 1917 he collapsed after having lunch with Rupert D'Oyly Carte at the Liverpool Street Hotel. He had passed away before a doctor could attend.

Bond, Jessie (d.1942)

Jessie Charlotte Bond made her first appearance as Hebe in *HMS Pinafore* in 1878, even touring in this role in America. She went on to star in *The Pirates of Penzance*, *Patience*, *Iolanthe*, *Princess Ida*, *The Mikado*, a revival of *The Sorcerer*, *HMS Pinafore* and *The Pirates of Penzance* and in *Ruddigore*. Her most memorable performances were in *The Gondoliers* and also in *The Yeoman of the Guard*. She was highly sought after and starred in many other long-running shows. She was full of admiration for Gilbert and Sullivan and for D'Oyly Carte. In her later years she entertained wounded soldiers and sailors but she died in Worthing on June 17, 1942; she was the sister of Neva Bond.

Bond, Neva

She was a member of the chorus between 1880 and 1891. Her first named role was as Isabel in *The Pirates of Penzance* in 1880. She also appeared in *The Mikado*, *Ruddigore* and *The Gondoliers*. She left the company in 1891 and made only two more appearances, at the Comedy Theatre and at the Lyric.

Bovill, Frederick

Bovill played Pish-Tush in *The Mikado* between March 1885 and January 1887 and also played the role of The Squire in *Ivanhoe* during the first half of 1891. Later in the year he played the role of The Chancellor in *La Basoche*, also at the Royal English Opera House. He made one more performance in the operetta at the Royalty Theatre, *A Hundred Years Ago*, in July 1892.

Bracy, Henry

He was originally engaged to play Prince Hilarion at the Savoy in *Princess Ida* in 1884. It would turn out to be his only performance for the company. He had already played principal tenor leads in a number of shows and he continued his career after *Princess Ida*. By the late 1880s he was in Australia performing in Gilbert and Sullivan operas. It is believed that he stage-managed *HMS Pinafore* in 1895, the first of seven Gilbert and Sullivan productions until 1906.

Braham, Leonora (d.1931)

She was born Leonora Lucy Abraham and made her first professional appearance in a revival of *Ages Ago* in 1870. She emigrated to Canada in 1878, but performed in *Princess Toto* and *The Sultan of Mocha* in New York between 1879 and 1880. She took the title role of *Patience* in April 1881 with the company and established herself as their principal soprano until 1887. She then left to give birth to her second child and they travelled to Australia, where she performed in a number of Gilbert and Sullivan productions. She returned to England in 1888 but was not part of Gilbert and Sullivan's plans. She did, however, go to South America and play a number of Gilbert and Sullivan roles across the continent. She also toured South Africa, performing Gilbert and Sullivan operas. She was re-engaged by the company between April and December 1896 for *The Grand Duke*. She then played Phoebe and Yum-Yum in *The Yeoman of the Guard* and *The Mikado* respectively on tour. Between 1897 and 1912 she performed around England and in New York and in March 1930, after her retirement, she was involved in the reunion with Jessie Bond and Sybil Grey of the original three little maids from school. She was living in poverty in a nursing home when she died in 1931.

Brandram, Rosina (d.1907)

Her real surname was Moult and she joined the company as an understudy for *The Sorcerer* in 1877. She created the role of Kate in *The Pirates of Penzance* and toured America in 1880. She became the principal contralto for all of the Gilbert and Sullivan operas for 17 years, from 1884. On the occasions that she starred in other shows they were largely unsuccessful, such as *The Lucky Star* in 1899. She performed in a number of revivals. The Savoy Company took *A Princess of Kensington* on

Rosina Brandram as Lady Sophy in Utopia Limited, *Emmie Own and Florence Perry play the two princesses.*

tour in 1903, after which she ended her D'Oyly Carte career. She made other appearances in 1903 to 1904 but began to suffer from pulmonary disease. In a celebration dinner of the revival of the Savoy operas in December 1906 Gilbert said of her:

> 'Rosina of the glorious voice that rolled out as full blooded Burgundy rolls down; Rosina whose dismal doom it was to represent undesirable ladies of sixty five, but, who, with all the resources of the perruquier and the make-up box, could never succeed in looking more than an attractive eight and twenty (it was her only failure).'

Rosina died on February 28, 1907.

Bromley, Nellie (d.1939)

She appeared in a burlesque at the Royalty Theatre in 1868 and later appeared at The Globe, The Olympic, The Gaiety and The Strand, before creating the role of the plaintiff in the original *Trial by Jury* production of March 1875. She was replaced by Linda Verner but continued performing in London, at The Globe, The Criterion, The Royalty and Drury Lane, until she retired in 1883. She was later known as Mrs Archibald Stuart Wortley and was 89 when she died in 1939 in Beaulieu.

Brownlow, Wallace (d.1919)

He began his career as part of a touring company. His first named role was in *Trial by Jury*. His first major role was in *The Yeoman of the Guard* in 1888, followed by *The Gondoliers* in 1889. He also appeared in Sullivan's *Ivanhoe*. After 1892 he worked in several comic operas and then travelled to Australia, starring in revivals in 1895 and 1900. Brownlow was known to enjoy his drink and was something of a womaniser. He tried managing a hotel in Australia but failed and emigrated to America. He appeared in three comic operas between 1904 and 1905. He was later brought back to Australia to perform but in September 1919 he succumbed to his drinking habit and died in Melbourne.

Chard, Kate (d.1942)

She made her first appearances as an amateur in Dublin and was then taken on as a member of the chorus in one of the touring companies in 1879. She left after a brief engagement and worked for the Carl Rosa Opera Company. She returned to D'Oyly Carte in January 1882, touring until the March, during which she met and married Deane Brand. They left for Australia, staying there for 18 months. On her return to London she took the role of Lady Psyche in *Princess Ida* in January 1884. It was a role that was originally intended for Leonora Braham but she had taken the role of the princess after the dismissal of Lillian Russell. Chard left the company for the last time in October 1884. At first she continued to appear on the stage, but then she and her husband tried management and production of their own comic opera, but it failed. She later appeared at the Royalty Theatre, in November 1889, and more comic operas throughout 1892 and then pantomimes from 1893 to 1894. Her last role was of the failed musical comedy, *Playing the Game*, at the Strand Theatre in June 1896. It collapsed after five performances, but she went on tour with it. She died in Shere in Surrey on January 4, 1942.

Clifton, Fred

He is believed to have been born in Birmingham in 1844 and was originally a musical lecturer and entertainer. He was engaged for the original production of *The Sorcerer*, but he is best known for his role of the notary in that opera and the usher in *Trial by Jury*. He also created the role of Bill Bobstay in *HMS Pinafore* between May 1878 and October 1879. He appeared in the first official production of *HMS Pinafore* at the Fifth Avenue Theatre, New York, on December 1, 1879 and also starred as the Sergeant of Police in the New York premier of *The Pirates of Penzance*. He then toured America until June 1880. It is likely that Clifton remained in America, as Rutland Barrington took over his role as sergeant in London. Clifton appeared in a number of comic operas between 1884 and 1887 in New York, including revivals of *HMS Pinafore* and *The Pirates of Penzance*.

Cross, Emily

She made her first appearance on the London stage as Diana Vernon in *Rob Roy* at the Theatre Royal Drury Lane in March 1867. She joined the company at the Opera Comique for the first run of *HMS Pinafore* and also starred in *Cups and Saucers*, written and composed by George Grossmith between August 1878 and February 1880. Harriet Everard suffered a bizarre accident just before the opening of *The Pirates of Penzance* in March 1880 when during a rehearsal she was hit on the head by a piece of scenery. Emily Cross was called in to replace her, with just two days notice, in the role of Ruth. She played the role until June 1880 and Harriet Everard was well enough to return. Soon after, she left the company and continued to perform in musicals and plays until her retirement in 1896.

Denny, William Henry (d.1915)

His real name was Dugmore and he took his first adult role in Dundee in 1870. He was taken on by D'Oyly Carte in 1876, but began his career

MR. W. H. DENNY.—In "The Yeomen of the Guard."

A caricature by Alfred Bryan of W H Denny in The Yeoman of the Guard, *dated around 1889.*

at the Savoy, replacing Rutland Barrington, in 1888. He would remain with the company until April 1893. He created William Shadbolt in *The Yeoman of the Guard*, Don Alhambra in *The Gondoliers* and Bumbo in *The Nautch Girl*, amongst other roles. He also played the part of Scaphio in *Utopia Limited* in October 1893. Denny then appeared at the Lyric Theatre and later toured with a Shakespearean company in Australia and New Zealand, returning to London in 1900. He performed in several productions in New York between 1905 and 1910. His last known appearance was at the Drury Lane Theatre in 1912, as Stuff, a theatre manager, in *Everywoman* by Walter Browne.

Everard, Harriet (d.1882)

After making her first stage appearance in Exeter in 1860, she appeared across England and in London in a number of comedies, light operas, pantomimes and burlesques. She starred in the role of Miss Partlett in *The Sorcerer* in November 1877, going on to be Little Buttercup in *HMS Pinafore* between May 1878 and February 1880. According to Rutland Barrington, whilst she was rehearsing for *The Pirates of Penzance*:

> 'She was standing in the centre of the stage at rehearsal one morning, when I noticed the front piece of a stack of scenery falling forward. I called to her to run, and got my back against the falling wing and broke its force to a great extent, but it nevertheless caught her on the head, taking off a square of hair as neatly as if done with a razor. The shock and injury laid her up for some time.'

She therefore missed the opening of *The Pirates of Penzance*, but took the part back from Emily Cross in June 1880. She then handed over the part to Alice Barnett. Everard left the company and never fully recovered from her injuries. She made one last appearance at The Olympic Theatre in January 1881, as Aunt Priscilla in Frederick Marshall's comic opera, *Lola*. She died in London on February 22, 1882.

Findlay, Josephine

After appearing in a D'Oyly Carte touring company in 1882 she was promoted to principal soprano and continued touring until 1885. She appeared as the understudy to Leonora Braham in 1885 and 1886. She took on the role of Zorah in *Ruddigore* in January 1887 and became Rose Maybud in the March. She then toured Europe, appearing as Patience and Yum-Yum until October 1887. At that point she left the company, but she would make another Gilbert and Sullivan appearance as Gianett in *The Gondoliers* on tour between August and December 1890. Her last known appearance was in the operatic comedy, *Miss Decima*, at the Criterion in July 1891.

Fishe, R Scott (d.1898)

Fishe was born in February 1871 and after appearing in the chorus at the Globe Theatre was taken on by D'Oyly Carte for the chorus of *Ivanhoe* in 1891. He appeared with the Edwin Cleary Opera Company in South America in a number of Gilbert and Sullivan operas from 1891, returning to England in 1892. He performed roles for D'Oyly Carte at the Savoy and in October 1893 he became Mr Goldbury in *Utopia Limited*. He then appeared in other productions before joining one of the touring companies in April 1895. He left the touring company in October 1895, coming back to the Savoy for a revival of *The Mikado*, playing the title role. He played the Prince of Monte Carlo in *The Grand Duke* and then did a tour of South Africa from December 1896, which included *The Mikado* and *The Gondoliers*. Illness forced the return in early 1897. After appearing once again at the Savoy in late 1897 to the spring of 1898 he contracted tuberculosis and convinced himself that he was dying; he committed suicide at the age of 27.

Fisher, Walter H

He was believed to have been born in Bristol in about 1849, making his London debut at the Court Theatre in 1872. He appeared in Gilbert's burlesque *The Happy Land* the following year. From 1875 he worked with the company on *Trial by Jury*, and later with the touring companies in 1883, 1887 and 1888. He was finally replaced by Frank Boyle in September 1888 and made his last performance with the company in 1889.

Fortescue, May (d.1950)

Her real name was Emily May Finney and she made her first appearance as Lady Ella in *Patience* in April 1881. She then played Celia in *Iolanthe*. When she left her role in August 1883 she became engaged to Lord Garmoyle but in January 1884 he broke off the engagement and using Gilbert's solicitors she successfully sued him for breach of promise, being awarded £10,000. She returned to the stage in March 1884 at the Court Theatre, as Dorothy in Gilbert's *Dan'l Druce, Blacksmith*. She used her settlement money to create her own theatre company, touring around and performing Gilbert works. Gilbert visited her on May 29, 1911, while she was recuperating from a horse riding accident. He said:

'Her appearance matters nothing. It is her disappearance we could not stand.'

In fact this was the very same day that Gilbert himself died. Fortescue would continue to perform in England until her last role at the Court Theatre, as Mrs Deveraux in *A Man Unknown* in June 1926.

Grey, Sybil

She was an understudy for the original production of *The Pirates of Penzance* in 1880. In 1882 she took the part of Fleta in *Iolanthe* and later played Leila. She created the part of Sacharissa for *Princess Ida* and appeared in the revivals of *The Sorcerer* and *Trial by Jury* in October 1884. She played the part of Peep-Bo, the third little maid from school in *The Mikado* for 672 performances. She then left the company for a year before returning in June 1888 for a revival of *The Mikado*. She remained with the company until the September and later she appeared in a pantomime at Drury Lane and a comic opera at the Prince of Wales Theatre in 1906. She was reunited with Braham and Bond for the 45th anniversary of *The Mikado* in March 1930.

Grossmith, George (d.1912)

After hoping for a career in the legal profession, he made his debut in 1870. His career really took off in the role of John Wellington Wells in *The Sorcerer*, which opened in November 1877. In March 1878 *Trial by*

Jury was added to the programme, with Grossmith as the Learned Judge. He played Sir Joseph Porter in *HMS Pinafore* and it was accompanied by his own *Cups and Saucers*. Grossmith played Major-General Stanley in *The Pirates of Penzance* for a year from April 1880 and then created Reginald Bunthorne in *Patience*, which ran at the Opera Comique between April and October 1881 and then the Savoy for 13 months from the October. Preceding *Patience* was *Uncle Samuel* for which Grossmith had written the music. He was exceedingly busy between 1882 and 1885 and became Lord Chancellor in *Iolanthe*, King Gama in *Princess Ida*, and then starred in revivals of *Trial by Jury* and *The Sorcerer*. He then created Ko-Ko in *The Mikado*, starring in it between March 1885 and January 1887 before becoming Robin Oakapple in *Ruddigore* for 11 months from January 1887. Grossmith then appeared in revivals of *HMS Pinafore*, *The Pirates of Penzance* and *The Mikado*. In October 1888 he starred as Jack Point in *The Yeoman of the Guard* and then left the company. He wrote and performed several sketches and monologues that were performed at Opera Comique or the Savoy. He entertained audiences accompanied by his own piano playing. He was granted a command performance for Queen Victoria at Balmoral in 1890 and in 1891 Gilbert asked him to write the music for a three-act operetta, *Haste to the Wedding*, but it closed after 22 performances at the Criterion. In October 1892 he began a tour of America and also collaborated with his brother in writing columns for *Punch*. Grossmith turned down the opportunity to play a part in *Utopia Limited* in 1893, but accepted a part in *His Excellency*, which ran between October 1894 and April 1895. He returned to the company and to the Savoy Theatre in February 1897 but he gave lacklustre performances and withdrew after just three appearances. He would appear twice more on the London stage; at the Royalty in November 1898 and at the Globe between November and December 1900. He died in Folkestone, Kent on March 1, 1912.

Gwynne, Julia (d.1934)

Her real name was Putney and she first appeared in the chorus of *HMS Pinafore* in 1879. She later appeared as Edith for the premier of *Pirates* in April 1880. She created the part of Lady Saphir for *Patience* in April 1881, staying in this role until November 1882, when she took the part of Leila for *Iolanthe*. She left the company and the Savoy Theatre in

February 1883. She was much missed by the company and for the majority of the rest of her career she appeared in straight parts. She married D'Oyly Carte's business manager, George Edwardes, who would go on to become one of the principal inventors of musical comedy at the Gaiety and other theatres.

Hasswell, Bowden

Actually J Bowden Hasswell, he was a member of the chorus for a touring company in 1887 for *The Mikado*. He was in the chorus of *The Yeoman of the Guard* in October 1888 and later appeared in the chorus for *The Gondoliers* and *The Nautch Girl*. His major Gilbert and Sullivan contribution was the creation of the part of Calynx in *Utopia Limited* from October 1893. He created his last role for a Savoy opera in Burnand and Sullivan's *The Chieftain* in December 1894. Little is known about his career after he was replaced in January 1895.

Hay le, John (d.1926)

His real name was John Healy and he learned his trade with a minstrel troupe. He was taken on by D'Oyly Carte in 1879 as part of the chorus for the touring company. He toured in August 1880 and March 1881 and again between 1882 and 1883, leaving the company in September 1883. After a season in pantomime he worked at several London theatres but returned to the company in August to September 1891, appearing on tour as Punka in *The Nautch Girl*. He appeared at the Royal English Opera House and then resumed a tour as Punka. In late 1892 he appeared at the Trafalgar Square Theatre in a comic opera and then in the spring of 1893 at the Adelphi in a drama. His last engagement with the company was in October 1893 when he created the part of Phantis for the first production of *Utopia Limited* at the Savoy, staying in the role until June 1894. After this he appeared at the Lyceum and the Lyric and then in New York. He toured America at least three times in comic opera and was on tour in South Africa for some 18 months. He was hit by a car near his home on November 1, 1926, after appearing at the Lyceum Theatre in the role of Florent in *The Padre*. He died the following day, after surgery.

Hervey, Rose (d.1899)

Hervey's real name was Sullivan and she was in fact Arthur Sullivan's first cousin. She joined as a member of the chorus in November 1877 and made her first Gilbert and Sullivan appearance as Celia in *Iolanthe* in October 1883, later starring in *Princess Ida, Ruddigore, HMS Pinafore, The Mikado* and *The Yeoman of the Guard*. She toured extensively as the principal soprano from 1889 to 1891. She left the company in December 1891 and she is known to have appeared in a pantomime at the Grand Theatre in Nottingham in 1894. She died in October 1899.

Hollingsworth, John

His real name was Hewett and he was believed to have been born in Reading, Berkshire in 1841. His first D'Oyly Carte role came in 1874 in a farce and then in a comic opera at the Opera Comique. He became the Council for the Plaintiff in the original production of *Trial by Jury* in March 1875, but he left in May that year to train at La Scala in Milan. It is believed that he was a cousin of Richard D'Oyly Carte.

Hood, Marion (d.1912)

Her real name was Sarah Ann Isaac and she had been a child star before being introduced to Gilbert during rehearsals of *The Pirates of Penzance* in March 1880. She was given the part of Mabel, which she would play until January 1881. At that stage she left to marry her second husband. She later appeared at the Olympic Theatre, the Alhambra and Avenue Theatres and later the Prince of Wales Theatre. Illness forced her to temporarily put her career on hold, but she returned to the Gaiety in 1887 and subsequently toured the United States. She was back at the Opera Comique in 1891 and her last probable London stage appearance was as a member of the crowd in court in *Trial by Jury* at Drury Lane in March 1898. She died on the Isle of Thanet on August 14, 1912.

Kelleher, Charles (d.1878)

Kelleher was born in around 1853 and had performed in operas and comic operas since 1872. He was the Forman of the Jury for the original production of *Trial by Jury* when it was on at the Royalty in March 1875.

By April he had replaced Pepper as the usher, but the Royalty closed in June 1875 and the company went on tour and he left the company. Kelleher rejoined D'Oyly Carte on three occasions between 1876 and 1877. Once again he appeared as the usher in *Trial by Jury*; this was his last appearance in a Gilbert and Sullivan production and his last engagement was probably at the Royalty in February 1877, in D'Oyly Carte's own *Happy Hampstead* in the role of the policeman. He died at the age of 25 on October 2, 1878.

Kenningham, Charles (d.1925)

Kenningham was born in Hull in 1860 and was a boy soprano. He made his stage debut at the Adelphi in 1882 and was later to star in *Ivanhoe*, *The Nautch Girl* and other shows. Although engaged by D'Oyly Carte for some time his next Gilbert and Sullivan performance took place in July 1895, starring in *Princess Ida*, *Utopia Limited* and *The Mikado*. He created the part of Ernest Dummkopf in *The Grand Duke* in 1896 and returned to the role of Nanki-Poo between July 1896 and February 1897. He then appeared in *His Majesty*, *The Yeoman of the Guard* and *The Gondoliers* throughout 1898. He was particularly productive when he headed for Australia in the summer of 1898, appearing in *The Yeoman of the Guard*, *HMS Pinafore*, *The Pirates of Penzance*, *The Sorcerer*, *Patience*, *Iolanthe*, *Princess Ida*, *The Mikado*, *The Gondoliers* and *Utopia Limited*, through to 1906. He died in Australia in October 1925.

Lely, Derward (d.1944)

His real name was Lyall and he joined the company in 1880, performing in *The Pirates of Penzance*. After George Power left he became the company's principal tenor and created the role of the Duke of Dunstable in *Patience*, Earl Tolloller in *Iolanthe* and Cyril in *Princess Ida*. He later played in revivals of *The Sorcerer* and *Trial by Jury*. His best loved role was as Nanki-Poo in *The Mikado*, from March 1885. He then became Richard Dauntless in *Ruddigore*. At the end of *Ruddigore*'s run he left the company, in November 1887 and then went on to perform on concert and grand opera stages. He was in great demand in London, mainly at the Drury Lane, between 1890 and 1893. He toured with Adelina Patti in America between 1893 and 1894 then toured with Richard Temple in

Rob Roy. He continued to star in a number of different operas before he retired and died in Glasgow in February 1944.

Lewis, Rudolph (d.1917)

Lewis was a member of the chorus for the revival of *The Sorcerer* and *Trial by Jury* in 1884. He created the part of Go-To in *The Mikado* and then created the part of Old Adam Goodheart in *Ruddigore*, Bob Beckett in the revival of *HMS Pinafore*, was back in the chorus for *The Pirates of Penzance* in 1888 and in his role as Go-To later that same year. He then created the Fourth Yeoman in *The Yeoman of the Guard* and was in the chorus for *The Gondoliers* in 1889. He continued to play parts for the company until the beginning of 1893. He did not rejoin the company until April 1900, appearing in a variety of different parts. He left the company after a tour in 1903 and then appeared at the Adelphi and the Lyric in London and seems to have reverted to being a member of the

Taken some forty years after its original production, Bertha Lewis as Katisha and Henry Lytton as Ko-Ko are seen here in The Mikado.

chorus. His last possible performance was at the Haymarket in 1912, in *The Golden Doom*.

Lugg, William (d.1939)

He was born in Portsmouth in 1852 and made his debut with a company in January 1884 in the role of Scynthius in *Princess Ida* at the Savoy. He later appeared in revivals of *The Sorcerer* and *Trial by Jury* until March 1885. He then left the company but would continue to have a successful career until 1927. He also appeared in seven or so films between 1913 and 1923. He died in Norwood, London on December 5, 1939.

Lytton, Henry Alfred (d.1936)

He was born in London in January 1865 and was married to Louise Webber, who stage name was Louie Henri. She joined the company for a provincial production in 1884 and Lytton joined the chorus, masquerading as her brother, at around the same time. By January 1887 Lytton was still in the chorus and an understudy to George Grossmith, who fell ill that month, whilst in the role of Robin Oakapple in *Ruddigore*. Lytton filled in to great approval. He won himself many of the Grossmith parts for provincial tours and played an enormous number of different roles in many of the Gilbert and Sullivan operas. Lytton was brought in as Grossmith's replacement in *His Majesty* and by now Lytton was extremely experienced and would play a bewildering number of different roles, not only in Gilbert and Sullivan operas but also other productions. He left the company in 1903 and performed in a large number of West End musical comedies. He reappeared as the Council for the Plaintiff in *Trial by Jury* in June 1906, later going on to play in *Iolanthe*, *The Mikado*, *HMS Pinafore*, *The Pirates of Penzance* and *The Gondoliers*. He rejoined the principal company in March 1909, touring all of the well known Grossmith parts. In fact he would continue to play many of the roles for the next 25 years. He was knighted in 1930, but he was severely injured in a driving accident in May 1931: he returned to the stage very quickly. His last known appearance with the company was at the Gaiety Theatre, Dublin, in June 1934 when he played Jack Point in *The Yeoman of the Guard*. His final appearance in any role was in *Aladdin* at Christmas 1934 at the Prince of Wales Theatre in Birmingham. He died in London on August 15, 1936.

Manners, Charles (d.1935)

He joined the D'Oyly Carte company as a chorister in 1881 and he was certainly in the chorus of *HMS Pinafore* and *Pirates* by 1882. He joined the main company at the Savoy to create the part of Private Willis in *Iolanthe* in November 1882 and then left, working with the Carl Rosa Opera Company, where he met the soprano Fanny Moody. They created their own opera company in 1897, putting on performances at Covent Garden, Drury Lane, the Lyric, provincial British tours, Canada and the USA and South America. The company was disbanded some time before the First World War and Manners died in Dublin in May 1935.

Owen, Emmie (d.1905)

She joined the company in August 1891, on tour, and as far as original Gilbert and Sullivan work was concerned she created the part of Princess Nekaya in *Utopia Limited*, which ran from October 1893 to June 1894. She toured with the company in 1895, playing the title role of *Patience* and starring in *The Gondoliers*. She was at the Savoy as Peep-Bo for the 1895 revival of *The Mikado* and created the role of the Princess of Monte Carlo for *The Grand Duke* in 1896. Shortly after this she left the company, returning to it in December of the same year and touring South Africa until June 1897. She then appeared in revivals at the Savoy in the summer of 1897 and again in the spring of 1898. She toured Australia and New Zealand in 1901, but had to end the tour due to ill health. She returned to England in 1902 and died at just 33 years of age in Kent on October 18, 1905.

Passmore, Walter (d.1946)

Passmore was taken on by the company in 1893, but his major Gilbert and Sullivan creation was Tarara in *Utopia Limited* in October 1893. From 1895 he would appear in a number of Gilbert and Sullivan revivals. His involvement continued through to May 1903, when he left the company and appeared at the Adelphi Theatre. He would continue to perform for another 30 years. It is believed that his last performance was in *The Damask Rose* in the role of Count Theodore Volney in 1933.

Pepper, Belville R

He was born in London in 1851 and Pepper created the part of the usher for *Trial by Jury* in 1875. He later became the Foreman of the Jury and then a non-singing part. He left the company in June, returning to *Trial by Jury* in March 1878, on tour with the Comedy Opera Company, also performing in *The Sorcerer*. The tour lasted until August 1878, and after this little is known of his career.

Perry, Florence (d.1949)

Florence Julia Perry was engaged by the company from 1890 to 1893 as part of the touring company. She was at the Savoy in November 1895 for a revival of *The Mikado* and later created the part of Lisa in *The Grand Duke* and understudied Julia Jellicoe in *The Mikado*. She also was involved in revivals of *The Yeoman of the Guard*. In late 1898 she travelled to Australia, appearing in *Iolanthe* the following year. She returned to London and made her last appearance at the Globe in *HMS Irresponsible* in 1901. She died in Durban, South Africa, in December 1949.

Pounds, Cortice (d.1927)

He was born in London in 1862 and joined the chorus of *Patience* in October 1881. Pounds would later appear in *Iolanthe*, *Princess Ida*, *Trial by Jury* and *The Sorcerer*. He played Nanki-Pooh for the American opening of *The Mikado* in 1885 and returned to England to rehearse for *Ruddigore*, but actually then sailed back to New York to play the role of Richard Dauntless between February and April 1887. He returned to London in May 1888, creating the part of Colonel Fairfax in *The Yeoman of the Guard*. He would go on to create the part of Marco in *The Gondoliers* and Indru in *The Nautch Girl*. He would continue to perform in London until he finally left the company in July 1895. He appeared in *The Yeoman of the Guard* in Sydney, Australia in February 1896. He continued to make regular appearances on the London stage for the next 25 years. He died of heart disease in December 1927. Four of his sisters

Courtice Pounds, who played Colonel Fairfax in The Yeoman of the Guard. *He was a tenor.*

appeared with the D'Oyly Carte Opera Company; Lily, Louie, Nancy and Rosy.

Power, George (d.1928)

Power made his stage debut at Her Majesty's Theatre on Boxing night 1877. By February 1878 he had taken the part of Alexis in the Opera Comique production of *The Sorcerer*. The following month he appeared in *Trial by Jury* and then later in *HMS Pinafore* and *The Pirates of Penzance*. He left the company in October 1880 and went on to become a singing teacher, assuming his hereditary title in 1903 and became Sir George Power. He was one of the four original artists that attended a reunion at the Savoy Hotel in 1914. He died in Kensington on October 17, 1928.

Rue la, Lillian

She first appeared as Hebe in the tour of *HMS Pinafore* towards the end of 1879 and then appeared at the Opera Comique in the same role, whilst Jessie Bond was in America. Later she starred in the first London production of *The Pirates of Penzance*, in April 1880, subsequently taking the role of Kate after Jessie Bond returned from the USA. She then joined the Carl Rosa Opera Company, undertaking British tours, including the title role in *Carmen*.

Russell, Scott (d.1949)

His real name was Harold Henry Russell and he made his debut in the United States in October 1890. He made his London debut at the Savoy in October 1893 when he created the part of Lord Dramaleigh in the first production of *Utopia Limited*. He also played the part of Mr Goldbury, filling in for Scott Fishe. Russell would go on to star in a number of other performances throughout 1894 and 1895, but he returned to the company in October 1895 as Cyril in *Princess Ida* and Mr Goldbury in *Utopia Limited*. He then created the part of Dr Tannhäuser in *The Grand Duke*, which ran between March and July 1896. After that he starred in the revival of *The Mikado*. In May 1897 he was in the revival of *The Yeoman of the Guard* as Leonard Meryll. He left the company again in March 1898, but returned to it in March 1902 as the principal tenor for the repertory opera company C, putting in performances in *The Pirates of Penzance, Patience, Iolanthe, Princess Ida, The Mikado, The Yeoman of the Guard, The Gondoliers* and *HMS Pinafore*. He left the company for good in March 1904, but continued to appear in other productions until 1907. He then took a three-year break and re-emerged with the Beecham Light Opera Company. Russell returned to performances in London in 1912 and performed in London and on tour for the next 26 years. He was the manager of the Lyric Theatre in Hammersmith from 1920 to 1932. His last London role was at Kingsway in October 1938, in *The Beggar's Opera*. He died in Malvern, Worcestershire, on August 28, 1949.

Sullivan, Frederic (d.1877)

Frederic was Arthur Sullivan's elder brother and originally trained as a draftsman. He was a keen amateur performer, but made his London debut in November 1870 at the New Royalty Theatre. He starred as Mr Cox in *Cox and Box*, written by his brother, at the Alhambra Theatre in October 1871. Frederic created the part of Apollo for the first Gilbert and Sullivan opera, *Thespis*, at the Gaiety, which ran between December 1871 and March 1872. After this he appeared in several other productions until March 1875, when he returned to D'Oyly Carte productions at the Royalty Theatre. He created the role of the Learned Judge in *Trial by Jury*, which he played both in London and on tour until late 1876. He died of liver disease and tuberculosis in Fulham on January 18, 1877, at the age of 39. Arthur Sullivan composed *The Lost Chord* in memory of his brother.

Temple, Richard (d.1912)

Richard Barker Cobb Temple made his professional stage debut at the Crystal Palace in May 1869. He appeared as Thomas Brown in Arthur Sullivan's *The Zoo* at the Philharmonic Theatre in Islington in 1875 and also directed the piece. He joined the D'Oyly Carte Company in November 1877, creating the part of Sir Marmaduke Pointdextre in *The Sorcerer*, performed at the Opera Comique. In May 1878 he created the role of Dick Deadeye for *HMS Pinafore* and continued working on other productions until 1879. He then played the Pirate King in the first London production of *The Pirates of Penzance*, which opened in April 1880, running until April of the following year. Then he created the part of Colonel Calverley in *Patience* but he did not make the move along with the opera to the Savoy, as he left in September, being replaced by Walter Brown. Instead he appeared as King Portico in a revival of *Princess Toto* by Gilbert and Clay. He rejoined the company to create the role of Strephon for *Iolanthe* in November 1882 and then appeared as Arac in *Princess Ida* and in a revival of *The Sorcerer*. Temple created the role of The Mikado of Japan in *The Mikado*, which ran from March 1885 to January 1887 before creating Sir Roderic Murgatroyd in *Ruddigore*, which ran until November 1887. Temple then starred in revivals of *HMS Pinafore*, *The Pirates of Penzance* and *The Mikado* through to September 1888. His next creation was Sergeant Meryll for the Savoy between October 1888 and November 1889 in *The Yeoman of the Guard*. He did not appear in the London production of *The Gondoliers*, but he played the role of Giuseppe in the Palmer's Theatre, New York production in February 1890. After this he toured in the same role, leaving the company in July 1890. He was back with the company for a brief period towards the end of 1891, touring in *The Nautch Girl* and then made several London appearances in different productions, including those at the Savoy, Lyceum, Drury Lane, Vaudeville, Olympic, Lyric, Shaftesbury and Trafalgar theatres. He made a brief return to the Savoy in early 1896 for a revival of *The Mikado*. Towards the end of the year he replaced Scott Fishe as The Mikado. He had no role in *His Majesty*, but starred in the revival of *The Yeoman of the Guard*, which ran at the Savoy between May and November 1897. In December 1898 he was Sir Marmaduke in the revival of *The Sorcerer* and from June to November 1899 he starred in the third revival of *HMS Pinafore* at the Savoy. He briefly toured in October 1904 in *HMS Pinafore* and *Iolanthe* and his last probable Gilbert and Sullivan performance was as Sergeant Meryll again in March 1909. He made far fewer appearances after this and focused on teaching and recitals. He died in London on October 19, 1912.

Thornton, Frank (d.1918)

Born in 1845, his first professional performance was at The Aquarium in an unauthorised production of *Trial by Jury*. He joined the company for the first production of *The Sorcerer* between November 1877 and May 1878. He was Grossmith's understudy and Richard Temple's understudy for *HMS Pinafore* from May 1878 to February 1880. Thornton created the part of Major Murgatroyd for the first production of *Patience*, which ran from April 1881 to October 1882. For *Iolanthe* in late 1882 he was Grossmith's understudy but he toured as Lord Chancellor and stage manager between February and December 1883. Thornton left the company and throughout February and March he stage-managed the first performance in New York of *Princess Ida*, at the Fifth Avenue Theatre. He then toured Australia for 15 months, playing leading roles in *The Sorcerer* and *Trial by Jury*. Thornton launched a second tour of Australia between 1888 and 1890. By June 1891 he was back with the company at the Savoy, creating the role of Pyjama in *The Nautch Girl*, which ran until January 1892 before touring, leaving the company for the last time in July 1892. His last appearance on stage may have either been at the Shaftesbury Theatre in 1893 in *La Rosiere* or he may have been the F Thornton that appeared in *The White Man* at the Lyceum in 1910. He died on December 18, 1918.

Ulmar, Geraldine (d.1932)

Ulmar was born in Charlestown, Massachusetts on June 23, 1862 and she made her professional debut as Josephine in *HMS Pinafore* in Boston in August 1879. She auditioned with Arthur Sullivan to play Yum-Yum in the first American production of *The Mikado*, which opened at The Fifth Avenue Theatre, New York in August 1885. She then toured as Josephine in *HMS Pinafore* in England and as Yum-Yum in Germany. She was then transferred to John Stetson, the US manager, playing the title roles of *Princess Ida* and *Patience*, and as Yum-Yum through to the beginning of 1887. She came to England to rehearse *Ruddigore* in the role of Rose Maybud at the Savoy and then headed for New York, playing Rose between February and April 1887. In May she returned to England to play Rose at the Savoy and then appeared in the revivals of *HMS Pinafore*, *The Pirates of Penzance* and *The Mikado*. In October 1888 she created the part of Elsie Maynard for *The Yeoman of the Guard*, which ran for 13 months from October 1888 at the Savoy. She then created the part of Gianetta in *The Gondoliers* and finally left the company in June 1890. She made other appearances over the next few years, both in London and on tour. After appearing as Jane Jingle in *Ladyland* at the Avenue Theatre in 1904 she retired from stage and became a singing teacher. She died in Merstham in Surrey on August 13, 1932.

Wilbraham, James (d.1921)

There is some dispute as to whether he was Charles or James Wilbraham, but the tenor's association with the company began in 1883 and he toured as understudy for the role of Prince Hilarion in *Princess Ida* in mid-1884. He was the associate in *Trial by Jury* in the October 1884 revival of *The Sorcerer* and *Trial by Jury*. He became principal tenor of the A company, featuring in *The Sorcerer*, *Princess Ida* and *HMS Pinafore*. When A company disbanded in December 1885 he joined the Savoy chorus and over the next six or seven years played a variety of roles in *Ruddigore*, *The Yeoman of the Guard* and *The Gondoliers*. He left the company in June 1892 and little is known of his career after this point.

Bibliography

Ayre, Leslie, *The Gilbert and Sullivan Companion*, Allen, 1972

Baily, Leslie, *The Gilbert and Sullivan Book*, Cassell, 1952

Bradley, Ian, *The Complete Annotated Gilbert and Sullivan*, Oxford University Press, 2001

Eden, David, *Gilbert and Sullivan: The Creative Conflict*, Associated University Presses, 1986

Jacobs, Arthur, *Arthur Sullivan: A Victorian Musician*, Oxford University Press, 1984

James, Alan, *The Illustrated Lives of Great Composers: Gilbert and Sullivan*, Omnibus Press, 1989

Jefferson, Alan, *The Complete Gilbert and Sullivan Opera Guide*, Webb and Bower, 1984

Smith, Geoffrey, *The Savoy Operas*, Robert Hale, 1983

Wilson, Robin and Frederic Lloyd, *Gilbert and Sullivan: The D'Oyly Carte Years*, Weidenfeld and Nicolson, 1984

Chronology

1836   William Schwenk Gilbert born, son of a naval surgeon, on November 18 in London

1842   Arthur Seymour Sullivan born, son of a theatre musician, on May 13 in London

1844   Richard D'Oyly Carte born, son of a partner in an instrument making company, on May 3 in London

1855   Gilbert at King's College, London, until 1857

1857   Gilbert joins the militia and begins work in the Privy Council office of the civil service. He begins studies at the Royal Academy of Music

1862   Sullivan's music to *The Tempest* was performed at Crystal Palace

1863   Gilbert is called to the bar and writes *Uncle Baby* for the Lyceum Theatre

1866   Gilbert writes *Dulcamara, or The Little Duck and the Great Quack*, for St James's Theatre. He also writes *Allow Me to Explain* for the Prince of Wales Theatre and another farce, *Highly Improbable* for the Royalty Theatre. Sullivan composes music for the comic opera *Cox and Box*, which is performed the following year at the Adelphi Theatre

1867   Gilbert's first *Bab Ballad* appears in print. He also writes and directs *La Vivandière, or True to the Corps* for the Queen's Theatre and writes a pantomime for the Lyceum Theatre, *Harlequin Cock Robin*. Sullivan writes *Marmion* for the Royal Philharmonic Society

1868   Gilbert finishes his legal career and writes *The Merry Zingara*, or the *Tipsy Gypsy and the Popsy Wopsy* for the Royal Theatre. He also writes *Robert the Devil* for the Gaiety Theatre and *No Cards* for the Gallery of Illustration

1869 Gilbert illustrates a second novel written by his father and the *Bab Ballads* are published. His *The Pretty Druidess* opens at the Charing Cross Theatre and he writes *Our Island Home* for the Gallery of Illustration. Sullivan composes *The Prodigal Son* to be performed at the Worcester Music Festival

1870 Gilbert writes *The Princess* for the Olympic Theatre (later this would be transformed into *Princess Ida*). He also writes the *Palace of Truth* and *An Old Score*, which is performed at the Gaity Theatre. Sullivan writes *Overture di Ballo* to be performed at the Birmingham Festival

1871 Gilbert writes *The Gentleman in Black* for the Charing Cross Theatre. Together with Frederick Clay he also writes *Ages Ago* for the Gallery of Illustration (later this would be transformed into *Ruddigore*). Gilbert is introduced to Sullivan by Clay. Gilbert also writes *Pygmalion and Galatea*. Sullivan writes *Te Deum* for the Prince of Wales Theatre and *Onshore and Sea* for the International Exhibition. Gilbert and Sullivan's first collaboration, *Thespis*, opens at the Gaiety Theatre and runs until Easter 1872

1872 Gilbert writes a series of comedies for the Court Theatre and also writes a sensation novel and *Happy Arcadia* with Clay for the Gallery of Illustration

1873 Sullivan composes *Light of the World* for the Birmingham Festival. Gilbert writes *The Wicked World* for the Haymarket Theatre, *On Guard* and *The Happy Land* for the Court Theatre. The second volume of the *Bab Ballads* is published

1874 Gilbert writes *Charity* for the Haymarket Theatre, *Great Expectations* for the Court Theatre, *Topsy Turveydom* for the Criterion Theatre and *On Bail* for the Olympic Theatre. He also writes *The Realms of Joy* for the Royalty Theatre and provides a large number of illustrations for the *Piccadilly Annual*. Sullivan composes the music for the *Merry Wives of Windsor* at the Gaiety Theatre

1875 Gilbert and Sullivan's *Trial by Jury* opens at the Royalty Theatre. Richard D'Oyly Carte creates the Comic Opera Company. Gilbert writes *Tom Cobb* for St James's Theatre, *Broken Hearts* for the Court Theatre and *Ought We to Visit Her,*

King Candules and *The Wedding March* for the Royalty Theatre. A volume of Gilbert's plays is also published

1876   Gilbert writes *Dan'l Druce* for the Haymarket Theatre and *Princess Toto* for the Strand Theatre

1877   Gilbert and Sullivan's *The Sorcerer* opens at Opera Comique. Gilbert writes *Engaged* for the Haymarket Theatre and *Sweethearts* for the Prince of Wales Theatre. Sullivan writes the score for *Henry VIII*

1878   Gilbert and Sullivan's *HMS Pinafore* opens at the Opera Comique. Gilbert writes *Committed for Trial* and *Foggerty's Fairy* for the Criterion Theatre and *The Ne'er Do Well* (later *The Vagabond*) for the Olympic Theatre

1879   Gilbert and Sullivan's *The Pirates of Penzance* opens at the Fifth Avenue Theatre. Gilbert writes *Gretchen* for the Olympic Theatre

1880   *The Pirates of Penzance* opens at the Opera Comique

1881   Gilbert and Sullivan's *Patience* opens at the Opera Comique and then transfers to the Savoy Theatre

1882   The Savoy Theatre opens with Patience and is then followed by *Iolanthe*

1883   Sullivan is knighted on May 22. Gilbert writes *Eyes and No Eyes* for the Gallery of Illustration

1884   Gilbert and Sullivan's *Princess Ida* opens at the Savoy Theatre. There are revivals for *The Sorcerer* and *Trial by Jury* and Gilbert writes *Comedy and Tragedy* for the Lyceum Theatre

1885   Gilbert and Sullivan's *The Mikado* opens at the Savoy Theatre

1886   Sullivan's *Longfellow's Golden Legend* is performed at the Leeds Festival

1887   Gilbert and Sullivan's *Ruddigore* opens at the Savoy Theatre and there is a revival of *HMS Pinafore* at the Savoy

1888   Revivals for *The Pirates of Penzance* and *The Mikado* at the Savoy Theatre. Gilbert and Sullivan's *The Yeoman of the Guard* opens at the Savoy. Gilbert writes *Brantinghame Hall* for the St James's Theatre

1889   Gilbert builds the Garrick Theatre and *The Gondoliers* opens at the Savoy Theatre

1890   Gilbert and Sullivan's partnership is broken after a financial dispute. Gilbert writes *Haste the Wedding* for the Criterion Theatre. Gilbert's book *Original Comic Operas and Songs of a Savoyard* is published

1891 Gilbert writes *Rosencrantz and Guildenstern* for the Court Theatre. Sullivan writes *Ivanhoe* for the Royal English Opera House

1892 Gilbert and Alfred Cellier's *The Mountebanks* opens at the Lyric Theatre

1893 Gilbert and Sullivan's *Utopia Limited*, or *The Flowers of Progress*, opens at the Savoy Theatre. Gilbert and Osmond Carr's *His Excellency* opens at the Lyric Theatre

1895 *The Mikado* is revived at the Savoy Theatre

1896 Gilbert and Sullivan's *The Grand Duke*, their last collaboration, opens at the Savoy Theatre. There is another revival of *The Mikado*

1897 *The Gondoliers* is revived at the Savoy Theatre and Gilbert writes *The Fortune Hunter* for the Birmingham Theatre

1898 *The Gondoliers*, *The Sorcerer* and *Trial by Jury* are all revived at the Savoy Theatre

1899 HMS Pinafore is revived at the Savoy Theatre

1900 *The Pirates of Penzance* and *Patience* are both revived at the Savoy Theatre. Sullivan dies in London on November 22. His last opera, *The Emerald Isle*, is left unfinished

1901 Sullivan's *The Emerald Isle* is completed by Edward German and produced. Gilbert writes *Harlequin* and *Fairy's Dilemma* for the Garrick Theatre. Richard D'Oyly Carte dies on April 3

1907 Gilbert is knighted on July 15

1909 Gilbert writes with Edward German *Fallen Fairies* for the Savoy Theatre

1911 Gilbert writes *The Hooligan* for the Coliseum Theatre. He dies whilst trying to save a drowning woman at his home on May 29